Still Hooked on Scotland

STILL HOOKED On Scotland

PAUL YOUNG

MAINSTREAM PUBLISHING

EDINBURGH AND LONDON

Photographs © Paul Young, Ricky Walker and by kind permission of
Diana Thornton

First published in Great Britain in 1994 by
MAINSTREAM PUBLISHING COMPANY (EDINBURGH) LTD
7 Albany Street
Edinburgh EH1 3UG

ISBN 1 85158 615 6

A catalogue record for this book is available from the British Library

Typeset in Great Britain by Servis Filmsetting Ltd, Manchester
Printed in Great Britain by Butler and Tanner Ltd, Frome

To my father, John, and my mother, Freddie,
who first introduced me to the delights of Scotland.

Contents

Introduction

This is a collection of personal reflections on the making of 18 programmes in the *Hooked on Scotland* series.

Along the way, I fished places near and dear, some new to me and others of which I had previously only dreamed. I met many wonderful people who all seem to share my belief that fishing should be about fun, friendship and enjoyment of the wonderful country in which we live.

My thanks go to all those who gave their time and help, encouragement, experience and friendship which allowed us to show Scotland in its true colours.

As in our programmes, there may be an odd hint or two and if they help you to catch a fish, I'm glad, and even if you are not too serious about fishing I hope you will enjoy this trip round Scotland with me.

Chapter 1

HARRIS

Voshmid at Last

It was a photograph taken by Arthur Oglesby that first fired my desire to visit Harris. His wife Grace, in the stern of a boat, is playing a salmon. She has her rod gracefully arched into a fish, framing an exposed mountain peak in the background. It was captioned 'Grace Oglesby plays a salmon on a Harris loch', and seemed to me to capture the beauty and starkness of the area. The picture appeared several times over the years, once with a slightly different caption actually naming the loch. So, I became aware of Loch Voshmid (or Voshimid) and for a long time fancied casting a fly where Grace had done previously.

When Harris was included as one of our *Hooked on Scotland* destinations, it seemed my dream might be about to come true. We were invited to sample the fishings of the North Harris Estates. We were also invited to stay in Amhuinnsuidhe Castle, built towards the end of the nineteenth century by the quixotic Earl of Dunmore as a grand hunting and fishing lodge. The castle's situation is as impressive as the logistics of its construction. It is built of sandstone, but Harris is granite, so every block had to be brought by boat from Glasgow. The furnishings, too, were taken to Harris from all points of Europe, fashioning a house of grand style in a very remote area. A salmon river tumbles to the sea in the grounds, and when the fish are running you can see them from the

11

Amhuinnsuidhe Castle and River

castle windows, splashing and jumping in the bay as they wait for rain to help them make the falls.

The fishings of the estate are set amongst perhaps the wildest countryside in Europe. The Forest of North Harris is bounded by Loch Seaforth on the east and the wild Atlantic on the west. The boundary between North Harris and Lewis is difficult to mark, but is somewhere between Airidh a Bhruaich and Bogha Glas on the A859 from Steornabhagh to Tairbeart. The fact that nearly all the signposts have names in Gaelic first, with the less expressive English underneath, is excellent. So many of the names were altered and diminished by the early map-makers, unfamiliar with the Gaelic, and it is good to see the historical names reaffirmed. Stornoway and Tarbert, Arivruach and Bowglass, are but the southerner's attempt at the Gaelic and less expressive for that.

Lewis and Harris are the one landmass at the northern end of the chain of islands making up the Outer Hebrides, but they each have their own characteristics. Lewis is open and rolling with so many lochs that, from the air, it seems like water linked by little bits of land. Harris, North and South, is more mountainous; a rocky east coast contrasting with the more fertile west, and the golden beaches of Luskentyre and Scarasta. North Harris is divided neatly from the southern part at Tarbert, where the east and west lochs almost meet, but for a narrow gut of high land. Clisham, in North Harris, at 799 metres, is the highest point. Now, I was brought up on pounds, shillings and pence. As well as feet. Using my Higher maths, and knowing a metre is 39 and a wee bit inches (point 34, if I remember rightly), this makes Clisham, according to my calculator, 2,619.3883 feet high. Let's round it off at 2,619 . . . and a bit.

We arrived at Amhuinnsuidhe with salmon in the bay, rain in the air and hope in our hearts. Tim Kirkwood took me into the rod room of the castle to explain the layout of the North Harris Estates' fishings. Some of the systems run north to Loch Resort and some south into the outer reaches of west Loch Tarbert, between Tarasaigh (Taransay) and South Harris. Guests basically come for the sea trout and salmon fishing in the castle river, the Ulladale system, Loch a' Ghlinne, Loch Scourst and its river running to the sea at Meavaig and Voshmid and its river going seawards north to Loch Resort.

After being shown the castle, Tim and I stood in the magnificent drawing-room, looking out into the bay. I remind you, salmon were jumping, there was a bit of a breeze and drizzle was in the wind. It was

Tarbert, Harris

The Voshmid sea trout hours before a meal was due, so I asked Tim what he thought we should do. 'Let's go fishing,' he said. Now, I have the will-power of a Kit-Kat, so when Tim suggested fishing and a visit to Loch Voshmid, well, who was I to resist?

We took the B887 back toward Tarbert and turned off on the private track up towards Loch Scourst. Bumping alongside a pretty burn in decent spate, I was in heaven. A shepherd drew us to a halt as he brought sheep off the hill for shearing. We made our way up the glen and came over a rise. On our left was Loch Scourst, with a good fishing wave purling the surface. 'Halfway there,' I was told. We bumped along the track and I awaited my first sight of this legendary loch, Voshmid. We broached high ground and started to descend. 'That's Weedy Loch,' someone said and then we saw this bonny but fairly small water. Some islands on it. Not remarkable, really.

'When do we get to Voshmid?' I asked.

'That's it,' Tim replied.

I was here, at last. Getting out of the car and having a look around, I saw Arthur's picture. Grace had been framing Sron Scourst (491 metres/1,609 feet) with her fly rod. In Gaelic, *Sron* roughly means 'Nose', and here I was, after who knows how many years, fishing Voshmid. My hands were shaking so much I could barely tie my flies onto the nylon cast. The tackle was conventional: 10-foot fly rod, floating line and a couple of flies – a wee Silver Stoat's Tail and a Soldier Palmer.

We set out in a freshening breeze, seeing the odd sea trout and salmon leap clear of the water. The first drift took us along the east shore among some little islands and skerries – perfect fishing water – and it wasn't long before there was a head and tail at the fly. Now, you are supposed to wait till you feel the pull of a salmon and be a bit quicker for a sea trout. It is not easy when you have adrenaline pumping through your veins, and of course I struck immediately. Thankfully, it was a sea trout, which dived deep and jumped high before coming to the net. They are beautiful fish, sea trout, and I was a happy man to have had an angling dream realised by this 3-pound bar of silver.

The freshening breeze freshened further. In the Western Isles, you are never short of weather and we were soon skiting down the loch at speed. Too fast for fishing and too hard a pull for the ghillie, so it was onto the shore, into the chest-waders and a-wandering the banks. There was one likely spot, near where the river runs out of the loch. A small dam had been built to keep the loch's water level satisfactory and there were large boulders lurking under the water – ideal resting places for fish coming into the loch after a hard run upriver. There was now a full gale whistling round my bunnet and it was a little difficult to control the fly, but just above the dam a fish took. This was a salmon which ran quickly towards the open loch and doubled back to the lie. It then ran across the rivermouth, jumped once and then again. On the second leap, it cleared the water by several feet and, blow me, landed on the dam wall! I scrambled from the water, almost falling in in the process, and ran for the dam. Neville Kidd, the cameraman, was right behind me and we must have looked a bonny sight as we struggled to reach the fish. But there it was, lying on the wall, my tail fly still in its mouth. I've heard stories about fish jumping into boats and beaching themselves on the far bank of a river, but in over 30 years of fishing that is the only instance where I've seen a fish jump out of a loch. And we were fortunate enough to have the

15

The salmon that landed on the dam wall

camera to capture it, otherwise I reckon nobody would have believed a word of it: 'Salmon jumping out of lochs? Away you go, Young, you're havering!'

That same gale brought rain and overnight the burns burgeoned into full-grown spates. Water ran off the Harris hills in all directions. The castle river was now in a condition for the salmon to try the obstacle course of the falls and the pools were alive with fish. Innes, our ghillie, was confident, if a little moist, as I cast a fly across the tail of the main pool above the falls. Fish were heading and tailing tantalisingly and it seemed impossible not to get a take: twenty, thirty casts and then a fish was on. What is it about that thirtieth cast that was different from the first, eighth, twelfth or eighteenth? As they say, until a salmon can speak, we'll never know. The fish charged about the pool, nearly leapt out of it (no dam wall here!) and the fly came loose. Try again. A small finnock took in fast water. Amazing to see that a wee fish like that will brave and lie in white water. But then we don't know what conditions are like under the surface. The lemonadey water on the surface may hide comfortable, unsparkling water beneath. But that is the wonderful unexpectedness of fishing. I did land a salmon later as the spate eased . . . a perfect Harris day etched forever on the memory.

We scooted around the Harrises, North and South, and found many delightful rocky points and promontories where an inquisitive shore angler might make merry. But as with so many places in Scotland, and especially the islands, lots are as yet unexplored. Take a map, sensible gear and there is opportunity in plenty.

Sea fishing too, is under-exploited – look at the map again and you can see many places that should yield good catches. We went out one wet night during 'Harris Week' on a gentle sea-angling competition. That great sporting fish, the pollack, was taken from kelpy lies, mackerel were there in plenty, some herring came to the teams of flies, and occasional oddities like gurnard added variety to the catch. All fish taken were distributed locally and the anglers with the best catches were awarded decent prizes. Excellent reward for a night of salty fun.

South Harris has fishing aplenty. At the head of Luskentyre Bay, Tony Scherr, manager of Borve Estate, briefed me on the genesis of Fincastle, a man-made loch at the end of the Laxdale River. Whenever you see the word or part word 'Lax', think salmon. German is *Lachs*, Danish *Laks* and Old Norse *Lax*. There are many derivatives – Laxdale being one of the most obvious, though oddly combining a mixture of Old

A 4-pound sea trout, taken in the dark at Luskentyre, with Tony Scherr

Norse and what sounds like genteel English (partially true: 'dale' does come from Old English, but is reinforced by Old Norse).

The dam was built last century, using local stone layered with peat. The entire enterprise cost just £200, and formed a barrier at the end of the river creating Fincastle Loch. The migratory fish have but a short journey to make from tidal water to fresh, and both salmon and sea trout are present in goodly numbers at the height of the season. We arrived the evening after the rains as the loch was settling nicely and Tony waxed lyrical about the sea trout. When the proprietors are not in residence, day-permits are for sale and if you hit it right, great fun may be had.

We set out on a greyish night, calm but with the possibility of fish. Tony told a delightful story of a man of the cloth, the Revd Smith, who was fishing one evening when a 5-pound salmon jumped into the boat (see earlier in this chapter!). It was recorded in the fishing book that 'after a short struggle, it was overpowered'. I suggested it might have been a difficult moral decision for the minister to make, a real question of conscience, but the fact that it was there for all to see meant that the good Revd Smith had no such qualms. As dusk fell, Tony hooked and lost a fish and I landed a decent finnock which Tony, having seen the fish jump, guessed at 1 pound 2 or 3 ounces. Usually very accurate, Tony. And as darkness drew in – real sea trout time on some waters but a bit late by Tony's reckoning for Fincastle – I hooked and landed a belter. Too dark for the camera to highlight out on the loch, we managed to show it to advantage back at the jetty: 4 pounds of fresh-run sea trout. My backside was soaked, the rain was dribbling down the back of my neck as we approached the pier, but I would not have swapped my place for anything. As Tony said, it had led me a merry dance. I am no terpsichorean, but those sea trout dances I liked. I was happy with the fish that led me my Last Tango in Harris.

Chapter 2

LOCH LOMOND

The Big Loch

Depending upon your point of view, I either saw the light or turned traitor when I moved permanently to the west, from Edinburgh to Glasgow. Until then, most of my fishing had been in the east or the Borders, and when I first entered the fishing-tackle shops of Glasgow, they offered permits for fishing in some places of which I had never heard. Cafaro Brothers sold tickets for Loch Lomond, of which I *had* heard, but the Endrick, the Leven, the Fruin or the Falloch were new to me. It was suggested by Charlie Mann of C.C. Mann that I become familiar with the initials LLAIA, the Loch Lomond Angling Improvement Association, and they very quickly came to mean something special. It seemed to me that here was one of Scotland's best-kept secrets almost on my new doorstep. Salmon and sea trout ran the River Leven into the loch and then up the spawning rivers; a variety of coarse fish were there in numbers, with pike running to 40 pounds and over: at that time, a Loch Lomond fish held the British record at over 47 pounds.

Since my defection to the west, the Big Loch and its associated waters have never been over-generous to me in numbers or size of fish, but who could quibble in such a place? This, the largest inland water in Great Britain, has around 30 islands and is dominated on its eastern

The Big Loch from Conic Hill

shore by Ben Lomond. I often think we anglers have the best opportunity to enjoy the overall beauty of the loch and its surroundings. We are there at different times of the year in all weathers, and from a drifting or slowly trolling boat the views of mountains and islands are ever changing. At certain times it can be rough and dangerous and at others there is a sense of stillness and timelessness, and you feel humbled by the fusion of so many elements into such a remarkable whole. You can feel the history of the place and sometimes when out on the loch, I thought about how the first sporting visitors fared on their visits.

For the earliest accounts of angling on Loch Lomond, we are indebted to Englishmen. Galling, isn't it? But they were made of stern stuff in those days – the earliest of those days being 1656. That was when Richard Franck and companion journeyed from the deep south by way of Carlisle, Dumfries and Ayrshire to Glasgow. On a fine spring morning they posted on horseback, taking the high road to Dumbarton where Franck and his unnamed companion were greatly impressed by the Rock. Even better news awaited them. Their pal, the commandant of the castle, greeted them with the news that after a month's drought, rain had fallen and the water was ideal for fishing. So off they went, the three Must-try-it-eers. Franck gives little clue to tackle, but does say 'I'm for the fly'. His companion says he is 'for any bait', while the good commandant fancies the worm: 'I perswade myself it will turn to best account, for the active eel, the dextrous trout and the incomparable salmon will greedily pursue a worm. Bring but a brandlin or gilt tail and try whether trouts be destitute of appetite.' They set to mounting their tackle and agree to meet after five hours on the water. Franck, fishing the fly, 'purposes to attempt the head of the Loemon' – the upper parts of the River Leven.

After the session, Franck is the last to return to the agreed rendezvous. They examine the catch. The commandant has some nice trout taken from the River Leven, not on the worm after all, but on 'nothing but a minew, some call it penk'. The penk *can* mean a minnow, but the name may also be applied to the samlet or young salmon. Could these anglers have been fishing salmon parr as bait? Franck's companion has two brace of salmon. He is modest about their capture, though, saying, 'Art was useless to catch such fish, as, careless of their lives, they cast them away. Look here, I have brought my evidences; this brace I caught, and this catch'd me.' Franck himself has done not too badly either. Two salmon and 'two brace of trouts that would make a Cockney's teeth stand a water and spring a leak' – whatever that means! But not a bad day for these pioneering chaps from the south, with six salmon and a good bag of trout.

A hundred and thirty years later, there bore down on the loch an expedition organised with military precision by a 29-year-old Yorkshireman, Colonel Thomas Thornton. Planning his 'Sporting Tour' in great detail in London in the spring, he and his companion, Mr P, set off towards the end of May. This was no day-trip. They chartered a boat to take the heavier equipment to Speyside and, as well as the crew, they had with them a falconer, a wagoner, a groom, a boy and a housekeeper. They took two smaller boats capable of being moved from loch to loch and some kind of tank was built for keeping fish alive. Nor did they stint on the food. 'Hams, bacon, reindeer and other tongues, smoked beef and pig' were laid in in sufficient supply to last until October. They took tents, six hawks, four setters, six pointers and a deer-hound; two double-barrelled shotguns, three single and a rifle. Fishing tackle was not itemised but they had nets of all kinds, pike tackle in variety and enough gear to accomplish any style of fishing over the duration of the tour. And one last bit of class: Thornton took with him an artist, George Garrard, to paint pictures of Scotland, which would be later used to illustrate the account of his travels. I suppose the modern equivalent would be a camera, which is fine but not nearly as opulent as taking your very own artist.

The expedition left on 6 June, crossed the border near Kelso four days later and headed for Edinburgh, where there was purchased 'an additional quantity of fishing-tackle, with six or seven excellent rods from that ingenious maker, McLean'. Then west to Glasgow for a week, a place Thornton knew well, having spent five years at Glasgow College. It rained heavily on the way to Dumbarton, where they arrived soaked but ready for dinner. The next couple of days were spent visiting friends, though he managed to have a cast or two on the Leven. Thornton had seen salmon jumping and sent his servant for his rod. The chap brought a trout rod by mistake, but the Colonel did get a few good trout in quick order.

The next day marks the start of some extraordinary sport. He was up at five and rode to the river where he got permission to fish. The river was well stocked with fish and he took five salmon before eight o'clock, four being between 9 and 22 pounds with the best a 41-pounder. Breakfast was taken and then they put out again on the loch to fish for pike. His servant had amassed a good quantity of parr baits (!), so a-trolling they went. A trout of a couple of pounds was taken first, probably a sea trout, then a pike of about 5 pounds. But the weather was too calm and sunny for fishing, so it was off for the shooting. A mallard and a cormorant were bagged, before another pike was taken on the row back to the inn at Luss for the night.

Over the next few days, many fish were caught: sea trout, or 'white trout' up to 7 pounds, a large number of finnock, small brown trout and perch, all of which were killed. Mr P set up a worm tackle and was quickly into fish, and Thornton himself was surprised when he took a perch on the fly, something most modern anglers have done at some point. On the homeward troll Thornton got a take deep and, after a strong fight, landed a huge perch. It was estimated to be about 7½ pounds – a monster. When they returned to their quarters for the night, the fish was weighed accurately: 'His precise weight was 7 pounds 3 ounces. He was very thick about the shoulders and I regret I did not measure him, as I never saw a fish so well fed.'

And if they weren't fishing, they were shooting and quite probably were often doing both at once, as the record for that day shows.

RETURNS

Shot six ducks, three seagulls, one scart, and one raven.

By trolling: one perch, seven pounds; one trout, six pounds and a half.

With fly and worm: fifty-seven trout and ninety-four perch.

A couple of days later they were off on the next part of the sporting tour, leaving the northern end of Loch Lomond by way of 'Cree in La Roche' – not too difficult to work out as Crianlarich. I'm sure the fish and the birds were glad to see the back of them.

This was around the time of the development of industry on the banks of the Clyde and its tributaries, and even when Colonel Thornton was taking fair numbers of fish from the system he was still moved to note that 'the face of the river here appeared much altered since I saw it last [only five years previously], nearly the whole extent of the north side being taken up with bleaching grounds, by which means the noble trout and salmon fishing there has been greatly hurt'.

In the two hundred years since then, we have perhaps gone full circle, with firstly the diminishment of angling alongside the increase in pollution inherent in industrial expansion, then the sterling work done since the Association was reformed in 1895, marking an improvement in catches which lasted until recent years. In that time, there were some memorable catches. Mr W.S. Millar of Balloch and his boatman, James Bain, in March 1912 landed a fish of 42 pounds. It took a small blue and silver phantom fished on a single-piece trolling rod near Balloch Pier and played furiously for over an hour. The skill of Bain the boatman countered the determined rushes of the fish, and it broke the record of Colonel Thornton's 41-pounder of 126 years earlier. But in 1930, Mr Edward Cochran from Paisley eclipsed all these big fish with a 44-pounder taken while trolling along the shore of Ross Priory. This, still the record for the loch, was again taken on a blue and silver phantom lure. Mr Cochran was 83 years old and his boatman, Thomas Hogg Junior of Gartocharn, was barely more than 16.

Then anglers such as Ian Wood, in his delightful book, *Out from Balmaha*, captured uniquely what fishing this great water was like just before and after the Second World War. And while he loved the loch, and

Trolling near
Balmaha

had some magnificent catches, he was aware of potential pollution of a different kind.

Nowadays, this wonderful water is suffering because of one of the main reasons for its popularity . . . its proximity to Glasgow and the Central belt. In my early days in the west, I loved the fact that I could be salmon fishing within half an hour of leaving my new home. I spent an afternoon and evening with Billy Connolly, drifting the islands on a bright sunshiny day. No fish, but a lot of laughs and a visit to Inchmurrin for a pint at the end of the fishing. We outboard-motored back to Balmaha, singing our heads off, with the hills round the loch sharply delineated against the summer night sky, and I got a row for being late home. It is impossible to communicate the reasons why one stays a wee bit longer than one said, unless you've been there. But that very accessibility has proved to be the loch's undoing. In these days of motorised access, people can bring high-powered boats, jet-skis and every variety of water craft to the loch with ease.

We met a real Loch Lomond fanatic one evening at Balmaha. Dave Sunman has fished the loch for many years and was kind enough to share his experiences with us. The salmon and sea trout come through the

26

River Leven and spread out in the loch along age-old routes. In the early part of the season, trolling is the recognised method of covering a large enough area of water to have a chance to intercept those spring salmon. As the season moves on, and the sea trout start to run, the keen fly fishers know the lies off the many islands and the best drifts in particular wind conditions. Dave knows that on these best drifts, you will have dark water on one side of the boat and light on the other. You drift that magic line where the bottom drops away. Sea trout like it about 10 to 15 feet and salmon that wee bit shallower, and on some of the island drifts you are covering a delightful mixture of varying depths where there is a chance of both species coming to the fly.

But that is the problem. These are often the areas favoured by the water- and jet-skiers. One jet-ski running along a favoured bank can push the fish into deep water and they will not come back. These are fish lost to the angler until the late season when they will run for their particular spawning area.

Dave and I rose a fish or two on our outings, saw Mayfly being gently sucked down by sea trout and although we landed no fish we enjoyed the ambience of summer evenings on the loch – before the scream of the jet-skiers spoiled the tranquillity. And Dave told enough stories of stoory summer evenings when only the anglers were out, with fish rolling and slashing at the flies, to make anyone want to fish here. And, don't forget, you'll be as likely to rise a salmon as a sea trout, and we all know that we should react differently to the take of each fish. Tighten into the sea trout slowly and give a salmon even more time. Easy to preach and difficult to practise in the heat of the moment. But that is what it is all about.

The loch is also famous for its pike. Mike Maule fishes Lomond often and I joined him very early one fairly damp July morning at a favourite spot, and that timelessness was again in evidence as we anchored up ready to fish. He put four baits out at different depths to intercept the pike as they quartered the bay in search of breakfast. What I find fascinating is the variety of baits a pike will take. Mike was fishing a dace, a couple of rainbow trout and an American brook trout, neither of the trout being, as yet, species found naturally in the loch. Loch Lomond has probably the broadest variety of fish of any loch in Scotland. Salmon, sea trout, brown trout, perch, pike and eel are well known, and there are also powan, minnow, stickleback, loach and roach. Mention has been made of tench and rudd and even flounders have been taken in the loch and mullet in the Leven. Modern pike anglers are often held responsible for the introduction of new species to the loch, but all the ones I've mentioned were recorded as far back as 1911 – though nowadays we might add bream and ruffe. The ruffe or pope is like a small perch and is a problem because it feeds on other fish's spawn, but Mike reckons it is mostly the coarse fish which suffer, the game fish spawning in the feeder streams which the ruffe, a relatively poor swimmer, cannot reach.

Anyway, Mike got a nice fish about 12 pounds on the dead-bait and we were discussing lures and how effective they are when Mike brought out the Big Bad Burmek. This was a large, jointed floating plug, red and yellow underneath and green on top. It looked huge but, as Mike said, it was really much the same as an 8-inch trout or perch from a pike's point of view. The action in the water was perfect, the tail section wobbling enticingly as it disappeared below the surface. And we were both amazed when, after a few casts, Mike was into a fish. At first he thought it was of modest size, but when it came close to the boat he reckoned it was not just a double-figure fish but a 20-pounder. I tried to get the net organised but was failing miserably, so Mike gave me the rod while he saw to the net. As I had the rod in hand, the fish jumped: a classic pike leap which Neville Kidd, the cameraman, caught beautifully; a moment, frozen on video tape, where you see the essence of fishing.

Unfortunately, the pike then decided to come under the boat and round one of the anchor ropes. It pulled free of the Big Bad Burmek and slid into the depths. Another of the great moments in fishing was captured as Mike voiced his disappointment, with a vehement 'Dash it'. The first two letters were actually redundant in this heartfelt cry as the fish disappeared from view. And I knew how he felt.

The dedicated band of bailiffs representing the LLAIA fulfil many functions. They will help, hinder and harry: help those who want to fish fairly and properly, hinder those who assume that they can fish without permission, and harry hard those who would bend the rules to their own benefit. Head bailiff Peter Holmes and his men will also help the shoals of salmon, and more especially sea trout, through the length of the River Leven on those wonderful summer evenings. Then, the fish can virtually be escorted from Dumbarton to Balloch and into the loch, passing on the way such potential obstacles as the Bonhill Bridge Pool. Here, a famous (or, perhaps, notorious) holding pool, where the British record sea trout of over 22 pounds was taken, may offer temptation to the less than scrupulous, but over the years Peter and his men have proved equal to the challenge. And out on the loch, the bailiffs work hard to raise awareness among those who might assume they can fish whenever they want, that they can't. The growing number of people afloat poses problems; casual trollers and the odd fly fisher aboard pleasure boats are gently but firmly made aware that permits are a must.

One September day on the Endrick, Peter introduced me to Arthur Hunter. I was privileged to fish his beat well above the Pots of Gartness after a spate had brought fish into the upper river. The 10-foot trout rod, 8-pound nylon and a couple of wee flies (a Jeannie on the tail and an Endrick Spider as dropper), proved that you do not have to fish heavy at the back end. Fishing from the right bank, shaded from the sun by trees, I had possibly the best couple of hours' sport ever. Salmon came to the tiny wisps of fur and hair, and in those two hours five fish were hooked and landed and another one lost. I was as amazed as Arthur and Peter. For once being in the right place at the right time, we got some super shots of salmon fishing on a small river.

Loch Lomond, its tributaries and surrounding country can provide anglers with rich pickings. But there are, at present, a variety of interests to be represented. For example, residents of lochside villages such as Luss abhor the noise and disturbance from motor-boats, water-skiers

The fly which took five fish in two hours

29

Two of the Endrick salmon and jet-skis which goes on until late on summer evenings, and we anglers agree that both are detrimental to our sport. But this is a large area of water, with enough for all to pursue their own interests. Surely we must find a balance instead of the present conflict, and I know many learned and committed people are studying these problems, hoping to find a solution.

I sincerely hope they do, as it would be a tragedy and a condemnation of our present generation if this jewel in the crown of Scottish angling was sacrificed. The ghosts of Richard Franck, Colonel Thornton and Ian Wood and the people who enjoy the loch today, such as Mike Maule and Dave Sunman, would urge that we further polish this gem, leaving for future generations a rich legacy – a big loch for *all* to enjoy, not just into the next century but for ever.

Chapter 3

MULL

Movies and the Minch

I first went to Mull to work on a film called *Madam Sin*, starring Bette Davis and Robert Wagner. The day I arrived, we were introduced to Miss Davis at ten past five in the evening and finished up by having dinner and long blethers with her and Mr Wagner until well after midnight. Mr Wagner was accompanied on his sojourn to Mull by Miss Tina Sinatra. As we were all passing reception one evening on our way to the dining-room, the receptionist called out to Miss Sinatra, 'That's your father on the phone for you, my dear.' She laid the receiver on the desk as Miss Sinatra went to the kiosk to take the call. The temptation was almost overwhelming. The chance to talk to a legend was there for the taking. I wanted to do the old gag and tell Frank to stop bothering me, but sense prevailed. That was the night I nearly spoke to Frank Sinatra.

We took our seats in the dining-room and amongst other items on the menu that five of us chose was 'A Vol au Vent of Neptune's Delights'. It so happened that we were seated near enough to the kitchen to hear our Glasgow-born waiter reduce this to 'Five fish'!

My second visit to this beautiful island was when we made the first series of *Hooked on Scotland* in 1991. As part of our programme on deep-sea angling, Brian and Duncan Swinbanks took us under their wing and

31

I was lucky enough to catch my first-ever skate. The fact that it weighed 140 pounds was thrilling enough and the hour or so it took to land gave me my first taste of what it was like to try big-game fishing. What was also interesting was that the chaps who had invited me to join them aboard Brian's boat, *Laurenca*, were fairly experienced in skate fishing, despite the fact they were nicknamed 'The Clueless Club'. There was fresh bait available in plenty but, somewhat perversely, I opted for a cocktail of a two-day-old mackerel and coalfish. There was a decent fishy pong coming off them and I naively reckoned this would disseminate across the sea-bed over 200 feet down, causing any skate nearby to lick its lips and go berserk with desire. The others were fishing a variety of baits – fresh whole mackerel or coalfish and any combination of both. Why that 10-stone skate, the only fish taken that day, opted for – talking cheese – the riper offering, I'll never know, but thank goodness it did. Next day's 60-pounder, taken on the same combination bait, was just as exciting, if a trifle less impressive in matters avoirdupois.

The Swinging Swinbanks, Brian and Duncan, know their waters well, having taken many Scottish records from Mull waters over the years. They are great innovators, too, always willing to try something that little bit different. There is always a chance of something spectacular happening in the waters between Mull and Coll and Tiree and north towards Muck, Eigg and Rhum – the Inner Minch. We saw the white-tailed sea eagles which have been reintroduced to Rhum, there are whales moving between the islands, and as far as fishing goes, well, you never quite know what might happen.

I was fishing for tope with Brian one lovely afternoon and we were standing at the stern nattering about the fishing when my reel sprang to life and line peeled off. It sounded impressive with the clicker on and I grabbed the rod waiting for Brian to tell me when to strike. Tope normally pick up a bait and run with it before stopping to turn it the right way round for swallowing. As they move off for the second time is when to tighten. But this fish just kept going. Not fast, but steadily and strongly. Brian suggested I hit it and I did. The rod arched and the fish calmly kept on going. I tightened the clutch as much as I could but it had no effect – the fish would not stop or turn. I had to give it line. Then all went slack and the fish was off. Brian and I looked at each other. 'That was no tope,' he said, and I thought he was probably right.

When the trace came up, we knew he was *definitely* right. The rod I'd been using had an 80-pound breaking-strain steel wire trace attached

Robert Wagner says, 'Hello Sailor'

Tope and teeth on light tackle

and we could see that it had broken a few inches from where the hook had been. The wire strands were all scratched and frayed and had sprung apart, now looking like one of those gadgets that chefs use to thicken sauces. This damage had been caused by something with sharply serrated teeth and into both our minds sprang the word 'shark'. Probably a porbeagle which to this day does not know it had been hooked. It was exciting while it lasted and the memory of it always heightens the pleasure of fishing Mull waters – you just never know!

When we decided to feature the island in our second series, we wanted to try something a little different as far as sea angling was concerned. Brian suggested that we try a species hunt, which I thought an excellent suggestion. It meant that we would be fishing in more than one spot, trying different baits and techniques for the different species. It would be a test for Brian, too, as he would have to use all his hard-earned skipper's knowlege of the marks where each species we hoped to catch might be found. But he is thorough, and the old ledger, full of squiggles and little alignment drawings as well as Decca co-ordinates, stood us in good stead. He found the marks and we got some fish.

Cod, pollack, coalfish, mackerel, lesser-spotted dogfish and the daily ling were all on the 'expected' list; poor cod and cuckoo wrasse a little more surprising. These were most of the species to be expected at that time of year, but Duncan and Brian reckoned an important one was missing; it was tope time again. An ordinary light spinning rod was set up with a couple of ounces of lead and a mackerel bait. The main line was only 8-pound breaking-strain monofilament. Granted the trace was heavier, but tope have sharp teeth, so it is wise not to be foolish. The fish Brian landed was all of 40 pounds and it probably only took him marginally longer to land than on traditional tope tackle and gave him much more sport. The fish swam off strongly when returned to the water, so everyone was happy.

There is a wonderful timeless element about sea fishing. As the boat gently moves with the swell, my thoughts tend to stray to other days on the water out from other ports and harbours. The fish I've caught, the funny baits with which I've experimented . . . the mind goes gradually into blinkers, when suddenly the rod top goes, a fish takes the bait and you are slap-bang back in the present. I love it.

Though we spent much of our time on the island sea fishing, Mull has more to offer than just salt-water excitement. There is trout fishing in abundance, for example. At different times of the season, Loch Frisa, long and narrow with a mixture of farmland and forestry on its shores, can give sport with trout of magnificent hue. Early season saw us trolling with some of Brian and Duncan's new Bridun lures. The trout seemed to like them as we took fish over 3 pounds. The fly works, too, as I well remember, when a fish came to the bob fly at that prolific conjunction of light and dark water, where shallow becomes deep, and broke me on the take. I'll never forget the sight of the roll of the fish as it took the fly, surged out of the water and broke my cast. I'd say 3 pounds, and who can argue with me? These Frisa fish are handsome, too, the larger taking on a silvery hue and reminding one of sea trout. As the year wears on, the fish, the big fish anyway, move into deeper water, but the fishing can be interesting. An occasional sea trout makes its way into the loch via the mile-long Ledmore River and the Aros River, so be alert; you will never know what is going to take the fly.

You can imagine how alert a certain James Greenhill must have been when fishing the Aros in a spate one late August day in 1911. I can picture the scene. He reckons there's a good chance of a salmon in the high water and threads on a couple of worms beside one of his favourite pools. He knows the fish are there and with a bit of luck this extra water will have geed them up a bit and put them in taking mood. He swings the bait out into the white water at the head of the pool and it comes round in the current – perhaps a bit quickly, so he adds a little more weight. This time he lobs the lobworms into the far edge of the stream and feels the weight touch and then gently bounce along the bottom. The cast fishes out and he tries again, a little more towards the far bank. The line cuts through the water, the weight touches bottom . . . and then that moment he'd been waiting for. The rod top nods and the line moves off slowly downstream. *Very* slowly, which is surprising as the small, active fish he usually caught tended to take the bait and run. No, this is a little different. Slowly but definitely the fish circles the pool. The angler decides the moment is right and tightens firmly. It is eleven in the morning as the rod bends into the fish, making little impression. Small wonder, or should that be large wonder? At ten past five in the evening, when the fish was landed by ghillie John MacColl, it turned out to be the largest salmon recorded on rod and line in Mull: 46½ inches from kype to tail, it weighed 45 pounds and is the record to this day. A cast of the fish was made and the actual hook and cast are also preserved. The hook would be about a size 6 and the gut cast around 12-pound breaking-strain.

*Mull miniature
railway*

There are some who say it was a fish destined for the River Awe, not really so far away, which had been drawn into a strange system by the smell of fresh water. When the spate had eased, perhaps the fish would have slipped back to sea and made its way towards the Falls of Lora, Loch Etive and the River Awe. We will never know for sure but the fact remains that this great fish was taken from this small water.

For those without fishing rods, by accident or choice, Tobermory in summer is a lively place to be. I'm sure it was lively in the late eighteenth century, too, when it was founded as a new port by virtue of its large, sheltered bay offering safe harbour to the fleet of herring boats. Nowadays, the bay is host to a different fleet, many of them holiday yachts stopping off for a night or two as they cruise round the Western Isles.

If you wish to tour on land rather than water, the car-ferry service from Oban to Craignure only takes about 40 minutes, giving wonderful views towards Ben Cruachan, the island of Lismore and Duart Castle, home of Sir Lachlan Maclean Bt, the 28th Chief of the Clan Maclean. Once on the island, you are likely to meet fishers, divers, bird-watchers or hill-walkers, such is the variety of pleasures available here. The weather can vary, but there is always something to do.

An evening can be spent at the country's smallest theatre at Dervaig, Mull Little Theatre; with 43 seats, it puts on professional shows throughout the summer. As if to mirror Mull being Scotland in miniature, there is the railway running from Craignure to Torosay Castle. The castle was designed by the leading Victorian architect, David Bryce, built by Campbell of Possil, and has Italian terraced gardens laid out by Sir Robert Lorimer. The mile-long railway, officially opened in 1984, was built and is run by enthusiasts who obviously take great enjoyment in the thrill experienced by their passengers. The journey, roughly 20 minutes each way, and tour of the castle will delight old and young alike. This old Young found it an hour of sheer magic!

South of the waist of Mull at Salen, the island opens out to the west. Loch Baa, Glen Forsa, Loch Spelve and Loch Assapol on the Ross of Mull cannot be properly explored in a month. Loch na Keal gives views out to the island of Ulva with the Treshnish Isles and Staffa beyond. The Munro, Ben More, dominates the skyline and, if you keep right on to the end of the road to Fionnphort, Iona is a short sea-crossing away. The great thing about Mull is that it is up to you to capitalise on its true potential, whatever your interest. For the fishers, there are nooks and

crannies where any angler with a wee bit of nous can find a burn enter-
ing the sea and adapt their techniques to fish for sea trout from the
shore. Inland lochs are well worth the effort for their wild brown trout –
permit in hand, of course – and there are many as yet unexplored marks
for the sea angler.

It is a wonderful place to spend a fishing holiday and to meet those
for whom fishing perhaps holds no pleasures. That is the thing about
Mull. You meet people who visit this beautiful island for the sake of the
island itself. The call of Mull is strong and I for one am always happy to
hear that call and answer it.

Standing on the pier at Tobermory after landing that 140-pound
skate, I was asked what it felt like. Many thoughts raced through my
brain. I was sore. My back ached, my arms were tired and my knees black
and blue from trying to keep my balance. It had been a long day, and I
had beaten my heaviest fish by the trifling matter of 121½ pounds. I suggested we go for a beer at the Mishnish so that I might be allowed to
gather my thoughts. With pint in hand, it suddenly became clear to me:
this was one of the greatest days of my fishing life. As I tottered back in
front of the camera to say so, I saw a Labrador puppy lift its leg on all my
fishing gear lying at the head of the pier. That is what I love about
Scotland and, at that point, Mull. It will give you great joy, but will never
let you take yourself too seriously.

Chapter 4

PERTHSHIRE

Piscatorial Perfection

Perthshire, perhaps, poses the perfect piscatorial problem. The sheer variety of fresh-water fishing available in this most beautiful area may give the angler delicious difficulty in deciding just where to start.

Talk Perthshire and most anglers think of the River Tay, but for a county stretching west to the wilds of Loch Ericht and Loch Rannoch, north to the old Devil's Elbow (now sadly gone!) in Glenshee and encompassing Lochs Tay, Earn and Tummel and rivers like the Tilt, the Lyon, the Earn and the Almond, not forgetting the Isla, Ericht and Tummel as well as many hill lochs and highland burns, it is obvious that there is a plethora of fishing opportunities for any adventurous angler.

Let's start with the River Tay. Everybody thinks of salmon, but sea trout, grayling, brown trout, roach and pike can also be taken from this great river and its tributaries.

The first day of the season for rod fishing for salmon, 15 January, is celebrated up and down the river in numerous ceremonies. The largest gathering is at Kenmore where the infant River Tay (a well-fed infant, I must say) issues from Loch Tay. Anglers gather outside Kenmore Hotel, one of the oldest in Scotland, and no matter how cold the morning may be there is usually enough bonhomie (liquid and verbal) to deal with the

RECORD TAY SALMON 64lb. LENGTH 4' 6. GIRTH .28. CAUGHT ON GLENDELVINE WATER BY MISS BALLANTINE 7th OCTOBER 1922.

Miss Ballantine's record 64-pound salmon

hardest frost. Drams at the ready, the piper leads the party from hotel to riverbank, where a quaich of whisky is poured over one of the angling boats to quieten the gods and render propitious the fishing season. That's the theory, anyway. Sometimes a clean fish is taken, though more often it is kelts that come to the spinners, and in recent years a number of large rainbow trout, escapees from fish-farms on the loch, have surprised anglers.

As a youngster, I always made a point of getting to Perth town water as near to 15 January as minor interferences, such as school, would allow. At the vast cost of 5/- (25 pence) per day, it was a privilege to be on the banks of this great river. Kelts were the order of the day, with some finnock coming to small Mepps spun close to the banks.

It was while still at school that I caught sight of my first Tay springer. An elderly chap had hooked it just below where I was fishing at the North Inch. The fish cleared the water on being hooked and the consensus was that it was a clean fish. The angler was remarkably cool about the whole episode and played the fish deftly to the bank. Not having a net or tailer, though, he was unable to get the fish up the steep bank. Another chap offered to hand-tail it out for him and stepped down to the water's edge. The fish was brought alongside, the expert tailer grabbed the line, gripped the fish by the wrist of the tail and heaved it out of the water. Unfortunately, he was still holding onto the line. This pulled the lure from the fish's mouth, the fish twisted and slipped from his hand and escaped back into the river. A moment to right itself, a flick of the tail and it was off. The old gent was remarkably restrained. 'Thanks a lot,' he said, reeled in and walked off.

Erstwhile expert tailer spluttered excuses as we all looked at him accusingly. 'It wasnae ma fault,' he whined. He probably *was* to blame, but I can still vividly remember the colour and shape of the fish. I got only a quick glimpse as it twisted out of whining tailer's hand, but the stocky build, full, powerful tail and violet, cream and silver flanks made an indelible impression. I often wonder what the old boy said when he got home. I know I would have been inconsolable, probably right up to the present day.

In recent years I usually dotter up on the 15th, not really to fish, but to renew old friendships. I particularly enjoy stopping off at Newtyle, just below Dunkeld. Elma Redford entertains half of Tayside, it seems, as car after car arrives for a blether and a chat. There is tea and coffee, sandwiches and sausage-rolls, soup and drams – but the jewel in the crown of Newtyle is the clootie dumpling. Warm, moist and delicious, the only way it could be improved is by making more of it!

And there is always a good chance of an early fish at Newtyle. The heaviest on opening day for the whole Tay system came from here in 1994, a cracker of 21½ pounds, caught by Elma's nephew, Philip Redford. I saw the fish and, though it had no sea-lice, it was extremely fresh and a fish to make anyone's season. Jammy chap, that Philip, a 20-pounder *and* clootie dumpling.

Despite the occasional good fish, Tay spring salmon fishing is a shadow of its former self. The runs of fish have deteriorated drastically and it is ironic to think that in the old days you had to take an autumn week to have even the slightest chance of getting a day or two in the spring. Nowadays, the situation is completely reversed.

I fish one of the lower beats one day a week from January through to the end of April with a band of fellow loonies, and though we do get a fish or two, they tend to come along when least expected and are indeed a bonus. I fished this same beat in the late 1960s and '70s and it cost 13 guineas a day. I had to save hard to be able to afford an occasional spring day, but it was well worth it. I remember Kenneth Bruce and I taking a springer each and Ian Letham being unlucky to lose one in a filthy rising river and from exactly the same spot in the Aitkenhead Dub. We thought things were going to be hopeless but, after a long trek to the water, decided to have a few casts. Kenneth saw a fish splash and covered it. It took a second cast and was duly landed – a sparkling springer. We were delighted that a fish would take in poor conditions, when we saw another fish move. Ian covered it and it took the heavy Toby immediately and just as quickly threw the hook. Still, two fish hooked was brilliant. We decided to sit it out for a while and I got my chance when that characteristic forward lunge of a running fish indicated another tenant arriving in the lie. Two casts and he took firmly. Landed shortly after, I was delighted with my 8-pound springer. We had done well on a day when most anglers would not even have put a rod up. I probably wouldn't fish a coloured water like that these days, but way back then there were good numbers of fish.

Nowadays on the same beat it is more for the chat and the laughs that we don the thermals and subject ourselves to the Perthshire 'spring' weather. It can be nippy out in the boat, even with proper winter woollies and neoprene waders, but it is worth the icy drip on the end of the

Polney, just above Dunkeld

nose to hear the chat of our ghillie/boatman, Douglas 'Bugsy' Stewart. He has fairly definite opinions on many matters and is not averse to telling all and sundry what they are. I know I've introduced him in print before, but like many of the chaps who work on the river day in and day out over the season, their views are always of interest. For the casual angler spending only a short time on the water, their advice and experience should be sought. You don't always have to do as they suggest, but it would be folly to ignore their help entirely. Bugsy always has a plastic container with, he says, the best Kynoch's Killers on the Tay – and the daily hire charge is very reasonable. Great fun and an amusing companion on the water.

As the season stretches, the summer salmon and grilse runs now have a better chance to enter the river by virtue of reduced netting activity. This will, it is hoped, let more fish into the system. Traditionally, a large number of these fish were netted as they moved up and down the estuary waiting for good water to run the river. If the reduction in netting does mark a significant increase in fish, those summer evenings for sea trout and grilse will be a pleasure regained.

And late spring and summer is the time to start exploring Perthshire. The hill-lochs are warmed up from their winter chill and are well worth a visit with a fishing rod. There are too many to mention here, but with Ordnance Survey in hand it is easy to enjoy a safe day roaming the hills and taking decent trout from a loch here and a burn there. Always check, though, that you have the requisite fishing permit and, if necessary, permission to cross land.

One hill-loch that we fished with the Scottish Ladies' Fly Fishing team was Loch Ordie, high above the Tay valley north of Dunkeld and nestling in the lee of Deuchary Hill. The loch is prettily set in the vast Atholl Estate and the trout fishing can be grand. Like many places in Scotland, it is not for the numbers of fish or size of individuals that one looks for on an outing to such as Loch Ordie. It is that magical combination of setting, expectancy and ability to fish well and wisely, and the fulfilment that comes with a happy conjunction of all three.

I've always been fascinated by how flies got their names. Who was it that came to this delightful water and worked out that a ginger hackle and white fore-hackle fished as a dapping-style fly would entice trout to come to the surface? And when and why did they decide to name it after the loch? Was that where it first brought success? Or was it just so named on a fly-tier's whim? And the Dunkeld: who decided to name it after this

43

ancient little cathedral town, beautifully situated in a richly wooded part of the valley of the Tay? Somehow the names seem right for these flies and they are well-known fish-takers. I'd be happy to have both on my cast at any time of the season on almost any trout water.

The larger lochs will, by summer, already have seen quite a bit of our old friends, the Ferox 85 group. No doubt they will have had a day or two on Loch Rannoch, trying for yet another British record brown trout (see Chapter 12 for the story of their capture of the present record). At the beginning of each trout season, there are probably more large brown trout taken in Perthshire than anywhere else in Scotland. The point where rivers enter or leave the larger lochs are successful places as the trout move back after an overwinter rest to recover from spawning. The first lure of the season through one of these pools will have a great chance of taking big trout, perhaps up to double figures. And don't neglect the larger lochs as the season wears on. Remember that the new British record rainbow trout was caught on Loch Tay by a chap out for a day's fly fishing. There have been many escapes from the fish-farms over the years and these fish seem to put on weight quite well in the wild. How they affect the indigenous species remains to be seen.

Rather like the ferox enthusiasts, there is a growing band of dedicated coarse fishers and Perthshire can provide an interesting challenge for them. We fished for pike in Loch Skiach, about 1,400 feet above the Tay near Kinnaird. Conditions suited the midge more than man: calm, windless and grey. We did manage to hook a couple of fish, but on the right day this water can fish well. As can Loch of Clunie, one of a chain of lochs on the road between Dunkeld and Blairgowrie. There are another couple of lochs of interest here. Loch of Lowes is one of the well-known nesting sites of that welcome summer visitor to Scotland, the osprey, and Loch of Butterstone is a delightful, well-stocked rainbow trout fishery.

But for many game anglers, as the year wears on, there is only one place to be – and that is back on the River Tay. As autumn approaches, the salmon gather in the estuary ready to make the final part of their spawning journey. This is a time of fecundity in Perthshire. The fields are heavy with crops, cattle are relaxed, sleek and well fed in the fields, and the hills are purple with heather as the trees take on myriad autumn colours. It is not easy to get a day on the lower Tay at this time of year, but even to walk the banks and watch the fish as they splash and roll in the river is pleasure enough. It would be good to think that anglers lucky enough to be fishing will exercise restraint and, in common with present thinking, return as many gravid fish, both cocks and hens, as possible.

The season for salmon ends on 15 October. The boats are out of the water for their winter overhaul. You'd be forgiven for thinking fishing was over for the year. Wrong! The grayling men are out and have the waters to themselves. This handsome fish is found throughout the Tay system – and good news, too, as it is a lover of clean, unpolluted water: a touchstone for pollution. Light tackle, tiny hook and a 1½-pound grayling in a fast Tay stream will give superb sport. This is a shoal fish and, once found, many fish may be taken. The true grayling angler returns all except perhaps one to fry in the pan in butter, relishing that delicate taste of thyme and cucumber.

So Perthshire can be enjoyed by the angler all year round. Over the years I've probably fished more in this area than any other part of Scotland. For anyone new to the sport, I recommend you buy a good map, several fishing permits and get out there. You have nothing to lose – except your heart to Perthshire.

Chapter 5

SOUTH UIST

Machair Magic

We left Glasgow on time and the flight to the north-west came in over the Little Minch where, from the air, Uibhist a Tuath, Beinn na Faoghla and Uibhist a Deas lay sparkling in the late-spring sunshine. This was my first visit to fish in these Western Isles and, seen from the aircraft, they resembled a brownish bracelet enamelled with a million specks of blue; in truth, myriad lochs with just the requisite amount of land around them to give access to this legendary fishing.

We also landed on time, collected the hire-car at the airport and loaded the gear. Driving south towards our base at Lochboisdale Hotel, we passed Creagorry and crossed from Benbecula to South Uist, our goal. East and West Loch Bee, on either side of the road, looked perfect as we passed, Loch Druidibeg Nature Reserve seemed a place to visit at a later date, but with what seemed like eminently fishable water at every turn, we persevered with our plan and met up with Captain John Kennedy at Bornish.

Conditions were good, so, without delay, John took us immediately back up the road to fish on Grogarry Loch. We parked the cars and walked to the boats. As Donald, the ghillie, pulled us away from the jetty, I heard a crackle from the reeds, the rasp of what sounded like a piece of wood being drawn across bone: the call of the corncrake. As we drifted slowly along the shore of the loch, patches of bright yellow contrasted vividly against the land. The flag iris was out. According to legend, the iris was first worn as a heraldic device by Clovis, King of the Franks, in the late fifth century. He drove the Romans from northern Gaul, was converted to Christianity and changed the three toads on his banner to three yellow irises. Six centuries later, the iris was adopted by Louis VII in the *fleur-de-lys*, which he wore in his crusade against the Saracens – *lys* being a corruption of 'Louis'. The plant, common on South Uist in late spring, is also known as the 'sword flag', as its leaves are sharp-edged and can cut anyone handling them carelessly.

The corncrake, too, is redolent of wild places. A visitor in summer, its numbers have decreased dramatically in recent years. Changes in the method and time of mowing hay may well be to blame. Last century, meadows were scythed later in the year, giving the birds more time to rear their young in the long grass. Modern mechanical hay-cutting now takes place earlier and also often leads to the destruction of both the nest and the sitting bird as well as a reduction in habitat. Though the corn-crake is now scarce, it is still to be found in the Uists. To hear its oft-repeated rasping call coming from the region of the yellow irises as a wild brown trout boils at your fly, well, you could be nowhere else on earth. Nor would you want to be. It is a comforting thought to know that within a couple of hours of leaving the hurly-burly of central Scotland it is possible to be afloat, fishing for wild brown trout on one of Europe's unique angling habitats, the machair lochs of the Western Isles.

Put simply, for the game angler, South Uist offers mainly loch-fishing from bank or boat for salmon, sea trout and brown trout, with the fly. But of course it is much, much better than that in detail. Brown trout in the machair lochs – those to the west side of the island – tend to come into condition in May and June, and the salmon and sea trout are to be taken from early July to October. And a bonus: fresh sea trout run the systems till the very end of the season. Nearly all the fishing is done with floating lines, so the angler sees most of the fish actually take; all in all, the apotheosis of Scottish island game fishing.

Captain John Kennedy is the fishery manager at Lochboisdale, a keen and knowledgeable fisher and the man responsible for easing the visitor to South Uist into the way of fishing on the island. At the hotel there is a rota allowing guests the chance to fish the best waters during their stay. If all the rods are not taken by guests, fishing is available to anyone willing to pay the fairly modest price for a boat. In May and June it is the brown trout which occupies the angler's interests. The machair lochs are world-famous. They are usually fairly shallow and rich in food, producing fat, fighting fish. Machair is sand-based, fertile grassland growing on a bed of crushed shell, close to the Atlantic coast of the island. In spring and summer it is alight with a profusion of wild flowers, a further testament to the richness of the soil. Feeding in the lochs is excellent; you only have to turn over a shoreside stone to see the wealth of food, and the fish readily regain condition as the water warms after winter.

Our evening on Grogarry was perfect. We took several trout and then John had a bow-wave follow his fly as dusk descended and a skein of geese honked its way overhead. The fish took the Clan Chief and leapt clear of the water. Moments later in the net, it was a perfectly proportioned, marvellously marked and wonderfully wild Scottish brown trout of about a pound and a half. I managed to land several fish, too, my first machair loch brownies, and as I slipped the last back into the water, Grogarry settled into late-spring late-evening gloom and a nightcap of

A beautifully marked machair brownie

49

cloud descended onto the peaks of Hecla and Beinn Mhor. A gentle row back to the jetty completed our evening. Well, almost, as back at the hotel, drams accompanied the tales of our and other anglers' exploits. That's one of the great things about Lochboisdale – there are always stories to share – and though it can make for a late evening, it is fun!

Then there are the salmon and sea trout. Come late June or early July and the first decent downpour, the burns running from the lochs are brim-full and sending messages out to sea: 'Come on in,' they are saying to the salmon and sea trout, 'the water's lovely.' And in they come, in goodly numbers. But that doesn't mean they are easy to catch. On Loch Bharp one breezy day I rose five salmon, not one of which took hold. We were drifting fast just off the shore, and the boils at the fly were sufficient to create a calm patch in the rolling wave the size of a double-decker bus tyre. By the time this had happened, the boat was over the lie and the chance to put the fly over the fish again was gone. On Loch Roag we were met with a beautiful day. Little wind, high cloud and lots of sun. The countryside looked wonderful but fishing was difficult and neither wet fly nor dapping could interest a fish. So, your chances of success here, like everywhere else, depend on getting conditions right. But in their heart of hearts, every angler knows that, and is willing to put with the unproductive hours because the productive ones are so wonderful.

The times when you know fishing is going to be less than successful, or on Sundays when it is respectful of local custom not to fish, are when South Uist should be explored. I've mentioned the corncrake and there are many opportunities for those with an ornithological bent to enjoy the bird-life, so now's the time to explore the Loch Druidibeg Nature Reserve. The west-coast beaches, miles of golden sand stretching from Grogarry south to East Kilbride, are where the Atlantic rollers first touch Scotland, and many species can be seen. These shores are great for beach-combing and can open the eyes to the vagaries of Atlantic currents. Fish boxes, glass bottles, lengths of rope and many unusual and interesting items are regularly washed up. American minutiae such as baseball hats, balls and even match programmes have been found tight into the shore, where the grasses anchor the dunes against the prevailing westerlies. Walking along these miles of unspoilt sand is a pleasure in itself; to do so on a day of wild westerly wind, well happed up against the cold, brings colour to the cheeks. And, as the huge Atlantic rollers crash ashore, their tops whipped to foam by the wind, you begin to have an appreciation of what our ancestors had to cope with in their quest for survival.

There are many antiquities to be visited: standing stones, duns and chambered cairns; or Flora Macdonald's birthplace, aisled houses and ruined castles – such as Ormiclate Castle, which took seven years to build, was occupied for seven years and then burned down when a roast of venison caught fire during a celebration of the Jacobite victory at the Battle of Sheriffmuir in 1715. Apart from burning castles and Flora Macdonald, there are many connections with the Prince. He actually spent a night on a small island in the mouth of Loch Boisdale before leaving for Skye.

There is a nine-hole golf course at Askernish (free to Lochboisdale guests) but, as I heard one local chap say, adapting a famous non-golfer's perception of the game, 'You'll perhaps not want to waste a good walk!' For the more energetic walker, this might be the time to try for the top of Hecla or Beinn Mhor where, on a clear day, though you may not be able to see forever, you might just catch sight of St Kilda.

Immediately to the south of South Uist lies Eriskay. One bright, sunny day I sat on rocks overlooking the love-lilt isle with Neilly Johnston, the ghillie. He told me the sad story of the demise of the SS *Politician*, the inspiration of Sir Compton Mackenzie's wonderful story, *Whisky Galore*. She was trying to get through the channel between Eriskay and Barra, took a wrong turning to the north and attempted to run between Eriskay and South Uist. Bad move. The shallow water and rocks drew her to a premature halt, and she foundered. Her cargo was mixed. Banknotes bound for the Caribbean, a variety of valuable commodities and, most importantly, some liquid assets, namely whisky. During the war it was difficult to get whisky; it was terrible scarce and any that was 'obtained', was deemed a godsend. Little wonder that when news of the tragedy percolated locally, these valuable assets were, as they say in financial parlance, stripped and invested wisely, and in the immediate vicinity – no offshore investments here. I'm not sure if many of the Caribbean banknotes found warm and loving homes, but, to this day, I'm certain any bottle of whisky from the boat will be sure of a warm welcome anywhere in Scotland; an investment that might give return well into the next century.

We dug a spadeful or two of bait and I waded out across the clear water and lobbed the bait into the channel. I wasn't greatly hopeful, but had a couple of wee saithe and a pollack in a pleasant hour. As the tide was one of the lowest of the year, vast areas of sand were bared and one woman was out gathering a real local delicacy, razor-fish, or 'spoots' as they are sometimes known. There is quite a technique involved, the details of which are a bit of a mystery to me, but basically you locate the oval hole and put your fingers slowly into the sand, and when you touch the shell, you grab hard. But you've got to be careful as they can move at some speed and the sharp shell can give you a nasty cut. Razor-fish, see? The spring tides are the best time to collect and this woman was an expert. She had a fair old sackful which she was going to make into a variety of dishes, including fishcakes which, she said, kept fine in the deep-freeze. She also said they tasted like lobster and very kindly gave us one or two to take back to the hotel. Nothing fazes the kitchens at Lochboisdale and they were duly served up that evening to be pronounced delicious by all who tasted them.

The sea fishing here, like many places in the west, has unexplored potential. On his day off, local Police Constable Donald Cameron took me out for an hour or two on the Minch side of South Uist, between Loch Boisdale and the small island of Stuley. For an officer who likes to fish, South Uist must be the ideal posting. There is not much crime locally, Donald and his colleagues being as much a presence as anything else. We fished fairly simply and caught species we would expect – mackerel, coalfish and pollack – with the odd surprise: a gurnard. We only covered a small area of water on a flat, calm day, and I'm sure that, like many of the more remote areas of the country, there is room somewhere for an adventurous skipper with the right-sized boat to explore and give sea anglers some excellent days afloat. But it is the game fishing that calls most anglers to the island.

Our second visit was later in the season when weather can change quickly and, with the wind freshening towards the forecast Force 9, it was a very different day on Loch Roag which found John Kennedy and I fishing from the shore. It was so rough, we couldn't get the boat out, but there was a good rolling wave and, if you think that the record sea trout for the island was taken by John from the shore in 1991, bank fishing is no great hardship. That was a magnificent hen fish of 14 pounds 6 ounces, beating the record of 14 pounds which had stood since 1965. Like so many of John's fish, it was taken on a size 8 Green French Partridge.

I had not long started, with fish all over the loch jumping and crashing back into the waves in a spume of spray, when one rolled at my fly. It didn't take and as I tried to put the fly over it again, I only succeeded in getting in a monumental fankle. As I was unravelling it, John was into a

fish, so I was once again cast in the role of ghillie rather than angler as I netted it shortly after. A slightly coloured five-and-a-bit-pounder, it was our only fish of the day and a fitting testament to John's knowlege of the water he loves so well.

Next day we were on Lower Kildonan, in John's opinion the best of the island's sea trout fishing. This is the loch where you can, at the right time of year, confidently predict that there should be a salmon or sea trout or two in the pipeline. The Roglas burn, running to the Atlantic and joining the loch with the sea, goes underground for the last part of its journey. There is a concrete tunnel, built at the beginning of the century, which carries the water under the raised beach created by the westerly winds and out into the sea. It was built to avoid the mouth of the Roglas being blocked by seaweed, the tangle of the Isles, and from half to high tide, the seaward end is well under water, allowing the fish to avoid the rush hour and travel to the loch underground.

Lower Kildonan is shallow and reedy and a large sea trout heading for the reed beds will provide the angler concerned with the best laxative known to man. The loch may be shallow, but it holds big fish. Sea trout over 10 pounds have been taken and bags of several salmon in a day are not unknown. My catch was more modest but equally welcome. I had risen a couple of small brownies when there was a savage take and splash and I was connected with a good sea trout. The weather was still pretty stoory so the fish was difficult to control, and being in shallow water I was worried that the droppers might catch on stones. But all turned out for the best as John's son, Ian, slipped the net under a glistening 2½ pounder. Straight from the sea, this late-season sea trout was a real bonus. Hard to think that shortly before it had been out in the sea and now here it was in the net. Just goes to show that even on South Uist, surprisingly, it *is* quicker by tube!

Chapter 6

SUTHERLAND

So Much Variety

Sutherland, the SuderLand or Southerland of the Vikings, is an area not just rich but positively wealthy in angling opportunity. Touching on the east, west and north coasts of Scotland, it encompasses large tracts of the last true wilderness in Europe. The coastline, sea-lochs and offshore islands offer varied fishing for the shore and boat angler and there are rivers and lochs aplenty with salmon, sea trout and wild brown trout.

I first fished in the west of the county on the trout lochs around Lochinver and Inchnadamph. It was there that I learned the thrill of dapping on Loch Assynt and also caught my heaviest-ever trout, exactly 6 pounds. It was also here that I spent part of a day fishing with two wonderful characters, A.K. MacLeod and Norman McCaig. The chance to fish with them had been arranged by Norman MacAskill of Lochinver and I fancied a go for trout in one of the hill-lochs. Norman knew the chaps were headed hillwards and negotiated me a place on the trip. I was at the meeting-place at the appointed hour when A.K.'s powder-blue Morris Minor 1000 with cream soft-top came into view. Introductions were made and we set off. The loch we were aiming for was Loch a' Ghlinnein, a stiffish walk uphill by the side of Allt an Tiaghaich. There seemed to be a problem, though. A.K. wanted to know

55

when we'd be stopping to wet our whistles. It was agreed that round about the 500-foot contour line would be fine. Next problem was whose bottle would be used for thrapple-wetting. Being the guest, I suggested that we use mine. Instant agreement. We stopped and poured a modicum of the water of life into our cups, diluted it slightly with the water of the burn, and took in the wonderful view as we sipped our water mixture.

Onward to the loch, another great sight as we breasted the rise and saw the water laid out in front of us like a rippled blue carpet. I was sent round one side and the two friends fished the other. Somehow, we got separated and I wandered the hill for the day, trying a water here and a water there. It is a wonderful feeling to be in the hills with trout rod in hand, and in Sutherland there are hundreds of opportunities to do so. The Stoer Lochs and those fished from Scourie would happily provide an angler with a different loch for every day of the trout season. It would be hard work, but it could be done. (Note: remind me not to suggest it to the producer!) Most of these are peaty lochs with few really large fish, but there is a geological feature throughout parts of the area which enhances anglers' chances.

Sutherland has some of the oldest rocks in the world, formed around 2,600 million years ago, but intruding occasionally is limestone, well known for softening and sweetening water. Feeding for fish is usually varied and plentiful in these more alkaline lochs, as seemed to be the case when I met Bruce Sandison on one of the famous Durness lime-stone lochs fished out from Cape Wrath Hotel. These waters are well known. Lanlish (or Lanish), Borralaidh, Croisphuill and Caladail bring anglers back year after year, and after my day with Bruce on Caladail I could easily see why. We struck it lucky, mind you. It was almost a perfect trout fishing day, mild with a decent breeze and a bit of cloud cover. There were gulls working and trout rising as we had a wonderful hatch of olives. The fish we had were not large but they were spectacular, jumping and running all over the place. And beautiful to look at – small head, deep shoulders and beautifully marked. A wonderful place to fish. I found it interesting that such richness exists in the most north-westerly part of Scotland, by geological fortune.

Less forunate in this part of the world is the sea trout. The popula-tions in east-coast rivers have not diminished as drastically as those in the north and west. The demise of this wonderful fish has been blamed on several things – from lack of feeding at sea due to overfishing of sandeels, to pollution from the many fish-farms now dotted round the

sea-lochs of the west coast. Whatever the truth – probably a mixture of many different causes – it is a fish badly missed on many waters. Loch Stack, for example, was probably the best sea trout water in the country in the 1940s and 1950s. Although there are still some sea trout to be seen, anglers who love this fish look forward to its return, sooner rather than later, to the long list of once great Sutherland sea trout waters.

A crisp Helmsdale morning – 'where's the river again?'

And the litany of famous salmon rivers in this county must make any fisher drool at the prospect: the Kirkaig on the boundary between Sutherland and Wester Ross, the Inver, the Laxford, the Dionard, the Borgie, the Naver, the Halladale, the Helmsdale and Brora and Fleet, and, flowing into the Kyle of Sutherland, the Oykell and Cassley and the Shin.

We visited the Dionard towards the end of June, early for the first runs of salmon, but were lucky to have rain overnight. A lot of rain; so much, in fact, that the river was unfishable until it started to drop and become that wonderful colour – like a decent cup of tea without milk. The pools above the tide and the Kyle of Durness, before the river turns under the road and heads for Loch Dionard in the shadow of Foinne Bhein (Foinaven), are worth a cast. I was lucky enough to contact a fish in one of those lies where you know a fish might stop for a moment after that initial run from salt to fresh water. I don't think I've ever had a cleaner, more sparkling fish. Fresh from the sea, it certainly made my day – a day of smirring rain and attendant midges. I was soaked through to the bone, bitten red raw, but a fish like that proved that there is always the possibility of a ray of sunshine of some kind on a wet Sutherland day.

But the Sutherland salmon river I've known best in recent years flows into the North Sea at Helmsdale. It has a justified reputation as one of the finest spring rivers in the country. Even that great authority, Augustus Grimble, introduced his appreciation of the Helmsdale (or Kildonan or Ullie, depending on which maps you read) with the words: '[it] is one of the best, if not the very best, of the early angling rivers; so much so that in the beginning of the nineteenth century, it is recorded that on the day before Christmas Day, 60 clean salmon were taken from the Manse Pool at one haul of the net'.

The genesis of the Helmsdale is two separate systems high in the forests of Achentoul and Badanloch which meet below Kinbrace. For the 20 or so miles to the sea, there is a delightful mixture of moorland flats, popply streams, rocky pools and fishy-looking runs. It is not a big river but, with the wind whistling round your ears, it is never easy to land the fly in exactly the right place. Grimble suggests the use of 'an 18-foot rod in early season, a 16-footer in April and in summer a stout trout rod is handiest'. In March, when I fish, I find the 15-foot adequate; a 20-footer would not disguise my casting inadequacies, whereas ghillie Johnnie Sutherland would seem to be able to cover *all* the water using a walking-stick with line attached. Dashed annoying!

The river is divided into twelve beats, six above Kildonan Falls and six below. Fish tend to run over the falls when water temperatures are in the low 40s – 42 degrees seeming critical – and in March the water is usually still cold enough to hold the fish in the lower river. Starting from the Falls, past the Vale of Tears, we reach the Manse where, remember, those 60 fish were netted on Christmas Eve, and the same place, again according to Grimble, where 'a Mr Rutherford, an old Helm angler, once saw six rods each with a fish on'. Nowadays there are only two rods allowed to fish any beat at the same time, though they do have the choice to fish above or below or both. The Manse is some pool, but I have yet to take a fish from it. The pool that has been kindest – and unkindest – to me is Upper Torrish on Beat Three.

I well remember a day when Mike Shepley fished Lower Torrish

with Johnny and his brother, Billy, and I wandered up to have a look at the Tail of the Bay. This needs a bit of wind and it was a bright, calm morning, so we opted for a cast on Upper Torrish, just below. I started in at the rough water, not usually a spring lie, and after a few minutes had a strong pull just off the far bank. The fish played dourly for some time and we both thought it might be a kelt. It then made a strong run upstream and there was the delicious possibility it might be a springer. Sure enough, we got a sight of that violet and silver flank and I whooped with delight as Billy netted my first fish of the season.

The traditional white hanky was waved to let the others down-stream know we had a fish, and we sat on the bank, revelling in the joy of the total experience: river, snow on the hills, and the wonderful quality of light in this part of the world as spring is bringing life to the land. I hadn't even fished the best part and we had a fish on the bank. Perfect. I checked the fly and went back in. As you fish down, the river is thrown towards the right bank, the one I was fishing from, by a shelf of rock, and it pays to let the cast fish right out – even allowing the line

Perfection! A 12-pound Helmsdale springer

59

to come inside where you are wading. There are big boulders there and you often feel a slight draw as the fly touches and pulls weed from the stones. It is a little annoying to have to check the fly after every cast but it is worth while, as the fish will follow the fly from the lies in mid-river and take on the dangle between those boulders. That is exactly what happened. I was slowly hand-lining back up when the line jerked, stopped and lifted from the water. I tightened and it was pandemonium. The fish took all the slack line lying in the water from the retrieve. It slapped against the rod butt as the fish turned downstream and had me out to the backing in seconds. It went straight down the middle of the river, then turned as quickly upstream. I had to hand-line like fury to keep tension on the line, helped a bit by the flow of the river. It came almost opposite me and, as I was getting some semblance of control, shot off downriver again. I stumbled from the water and up the bank, trying to follow the fish. Lower Torrish is a long pool and widens near the tail, so a fish running downstream and towards the far bank can take a lot of line from the reel. At more than one point in the fight, my entire fly-line and not a little backing were submerged as the fish ran this way and that. After a few minutes, things settled down and I managed to get the fly-line back on the reel and appeared to be in control. The fish slowly came towards our bank and, at length, the join of cast and fly-line came out of the water at my feet. We still had not seen the fish, but knew it was substantial. More of the cast appeared and, as the fish swam past, I got the faintest sighting in the golden, peaty water. I also saw a swirl some long distance behind where the cast was veeing through the water. I knew that a couple of fish over 20 pounds had been taken from the river in the past few days and I was sure this might be one of similar size. As the fish again came lazily past our feet, the fly gently popped out of the water and the fish was gone. Billy and I looked at each other. Nothing was said.

I wound in, hooked the fly under the reel seat and laid the rod down on the riverbank. I wandered off towards an old sheep stall near the river, sat on the wall and pondered. I'd lost what might have been my first-ever 20-pounder, and a springer at that. The train from Thurso to Inverness came down the strath and people aboard waved from the windows. I waved back. That helped me come to terms with what had happened. At least I had already landed a fish. And of the other, as Isaac Walton says in *The Compleat Angler*, one cannot say one has 'lost' a fish, as you cannot lose that which you never had.

Over the ten years or so that I have fished this wonderful water, I've never really been in 'the right place at the right time'. March used to be a great month, but has proved a little difficult in recent years. No matter. I still love the total ambience of that part of Sutherland in early spring.

Mind you, it was no easier when we tried the town water in summer. Daily permits are available for the lower stretch and, with enough water, good catches of salmon and sea trout can be taken. I tried dibbling – dancing the dropper in broken water, streamy runs or white water created as the river runs over and between boulders – but to no avail. I saw fish, fresh fish too, but they were running upriver fast and not keen to pause and dally with the dibble. Bars of silver, these fish were; unable to entice them, it was suggested I try for bars of gold – panning the river and its tributaries like prospectors did in Sutherland over a hundred years ago.

The story of the Kildonan Gold Rush goes back to 1868 when Mr R. Gilchrist, a native of Strath Kildonan, returned home after 17 years in the Australian goldfields. He knew that 50 years earlier, a single nugget weighing 15 grams had been found in the River Helmsdale. It was fashioned into a ring for the Duke of Sutherland, so Mr Gilchrist applied to the Duke for permission to pan. It is said he started the search above the bridge at Helmsdale and worked his way upstream. He found gold and went on to search the river's tributaries, finding the best in the Suisgill Burn. News of his discoveries spread quickly, and soon the river-banks were alive with prospectors.

The next year the Duke decided to bring some order to the enterprise by allocating plots of 40 square feet per person at a licence fee of one pound for each month, plus 10 per cent of all gold retrieved. One pound a month was a fair sum back in 1869, and most prospectors would hope that they found enough gold to pay for the following month's licence. By now there were about five hundred panners at work and a village had sprung up beside the Kildonan Burn, though some lived rough on their individual claims. Helmsdale prospered as gold was used to buy food and drink, rather than have the Duke take his percentage. It is said that about twelve thousand pounds of gold was taken from the various sites and the Duke was so happy with the whole enterprise that he threw a big dinner for the miners, with Mr Gilchrist as guest of honour.

The growing band of hopefuls spread their activities wider: north into Caithness and south to the Brora; but problems loomed. The deer were being driven off the estates, the salmon fishing was suffering (would that we could use that excuse these days!), and farmers were complaining that their sheep had nowhere to lamb without being disturbed by the prospectors. So, perhaps reluctantly, the Duke withdrew the licences and his permission, and on 1 January 1870, just two years after it started, the Gold Rush was over. But as with the bars of silver, the salmon, there were those who poached for their bars of gold. It is said that nocturnal activity was high; ghostly figures making for the best panning areas, such as Suisgill Burn, under cover of darkness and taking away sacks of stone and gravel to be washed at their leisure during daylight hours well away from the river.

There is still gold in the area today. You can apply for a free permit and pan to your heart's content, as long as you keep within the designated area, away from the main river and the salmon spawning-beds. The people we met near Baile-nan-Or (what was once the Town of Gold) enjoy gold panning as a healthy outdoor hobby, and over the years have amassed varying quantities – in some cases enough to have rings made for themselves and their families.

During the prospecting in those couple of years long ago, living was pretty harsh in the makeshift village, and at Timespan Heritage Centre in Helmsdale there is an exhibition illustrating life in this part of Sutherland, then and through the centuries. It is a stark reminder of all the hardships people had to bear and a compliment to their hardiness and fortitude.

Opposite Timespan is La Mirage. What can one say about this, 'The North's Premier Restaurant'? Nancy Sinclair has created a haven of peace and colour, where good food goes hand-in-hand with a warm welcome, whatever time of day or evening. Her son, Donald, makes the best battered haddock you'll ever taste and he'll run you up a dozen scones or sugared doughnuts at the drop of his chef's hat. Nancy is not one for understatement, whether it be the interior decoration (pink, with sun umbrellas over the tables) or the varieties of colourful nail-varnish she uses. It is even said that on special occasions she'll put on the tartan nail-polish!

Nancy is often mistaken for one of Helmsdale's more kenspeckle visitors, Dame Barbara Cartland, a regular visitor here since the 1920s. She talked to us in the garden of Kilphedir Lodge, overlooking the river. She first tried fishing for salmon in 1927, and on her initial foray caught four fish and lost five. She wondered what all the fuss was about – why

With Dame Barbara Cartland at Kilphedir Lodge on the River Helmsdale

people had said it was so difficult – but as with so many anglers before and since, it was never so easy after, and that first day has seldom been matched. She fished regularly over the years and reckons that she has had about two hundred salmon. Not bad going, when you consider that she might have been writing several novels at the same time.

For a long time, the west coast of Sutherland has been a popular area for the sea angler. Norman MacAskill and others have had halibut and skate out from Lochinver, and there are many marks where the more usual species can be taken, whether by the serious angler or someone on holiday just wanting a couple of hours on the water. As we did with Alex Jappy for cod out from Helmsdale harbour, and with Ewen Shairp for pollack (and, as it happened, octopus) out from Lochinver. The number of octopus we caught surprised some, but they are often taken in the pots and are good bait for a variety of fish – and delicious to eat, prepared properly.

So, Sutherland has much to offer and in our half-hour programme we could really only touch on some aspects of interest to the angler. The best way to get a feel for the place is to fish a hill-loch in late May, try for sea trout on a July evening and salmon at daybreak the next morning, or have a sunny day sea fishing in August. You'll learn to recognise Suilven and Stac Polly, Quinag and Arkle, marvel at the vistas to be seen all over the county and, like the Vikings all those years ago, you'll come back again and again.

A fine halibut taken from Norman MacAskill's boat out from Lochinver

A beautifully shaped Loch Frisa trout

The Upper Tay in all its splendour

Flag irises on Uist

The bridge at Kenmore, where loch becomes river

South Uist – 'a brownish bracelet enamelled with a million specks of blue'

Rainbow over Tweed

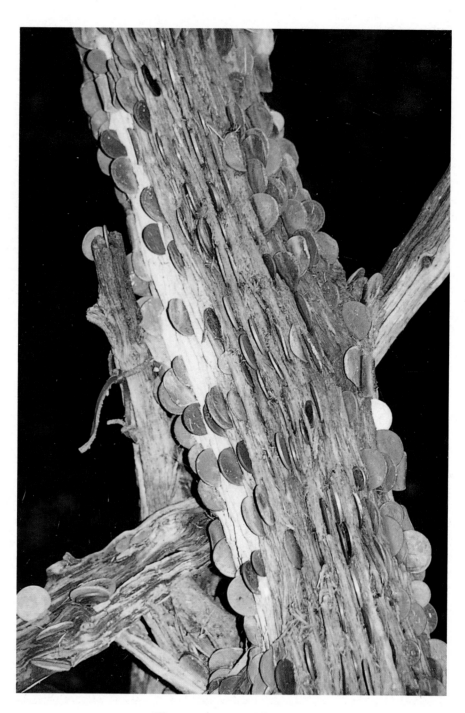

The money tree on Isle Maree

Orcadian flavours

Rainbow bunnet

Plowtering in the Palnackie mud with Harry Ellis

*A delighted Alasdair Thorne with the new British record brown trout, of 19
pounds 12 ounces, from Loch Awe*

Chapter 7

KELSO AND LOWER TWEED

Dreams Realised

As a youngster becoming aware of fishing, I had two dreams. I longed to catch a trout of a pound and a salmon of 20. Certainly the former was likely to be the more attainable, but it is interesting that both of these angling milestones were reached on the banks of the river with which, over the years, I had become most familiar: the Tweed.

I mentioned in the first *Hooked on Scotland* book, that my mother's side of the family comes from the Borders and that at an early age I was often taken by my Uncle Hendy on trips all round the area. In those days, the Tweed was a great trout river. In springtime, not long after the season opened, there would be great hatches of March Browns, the first fly of the year to come onto the water and offer the chance for trout to feed themselves back into condition after spawning and winter. There were, at the height of the hatches, literally rafts of big flies fluttering down-river, and the trout took no little advantage of these meals on wings. It seemed impossible that a fish would prefer the man-made version to the natural, but every now and then a neb would poke through the surface, suck down the imitation and another bonny Tweed trout would come to the net. Later in the season there were hatches of olives and many other naturals, and, apart from the March Brown, two other flies became firm favourite trout-takers, the Greenwell and Tup's Indispensable.

The Greenwell . . . Greenwell's Glory. Since its invention, there are few anglers who would be brave enough to venture fishing anywhere in Scotland without at least one version of this wonderful fly in their box. The fancy of the good Canon William Greenwell, it was first tied by John Wright of Kelso to the Canon's instructions as an olive imitation. A simple fly, the secret perhaps of its success, and to this day still basically tied very much to the original pattern: primrose silk, ribbed with fine gold wire and furnace hackle. Canon Greenwell, born in 1820, was vicar of Lanchester, between Consett and Durham, and became canon and librarian of Durham Cathedral. He travelled much in the north of England and, being a keen angler, obviously made many forays over the border. An inveterate collector of artefacts, he surely had an educated eye for detail and this led him to ask Mr Wright to tie up a wet fly to the specifications already set out. Mr Wright did so and, on the first time of its use, the fly was highly successful. Indeed, at a dinner to celebrate the large basket of fish it beguiled, the fly itself received the honour of a toast: 'Here's to Greenwell's Glory,' someone said and we are still saying it to this day. In a letter to a friend in 1912, Canon Greenwell described his season. He had taken exactly one hundred trout with a total weight of 117 pounds. An average over a pound anywhere is not bad but is even better if you consider he was then 92 years old. In his latter years he was to be seen fishing from a bath-chair on the riverbank. He passed away peacefully in 1918, a few weeks before his 98th birthday.

Tup's Indispensable was the other fly that did well for Uncle Hendy on the Tweed, usually the dry fly fished on summer evenings. But even as late as the 1930s, there was a mystique about the correct dressing for it. It seems that the fly was the invention of a Mr Austin from Tiverton who ran a fishing-tackle shop. The fly was one of his bestsellers and, quite rightly, he kept the details of how it was tied as a trade secret. Even after his death, his daughter Agnes held on to that secret until the 1950s, when the mystery was solved. We might know from the name that the male sheep is involved somewhere, but I was a little surprised that the secret that Agnes held on to for so long (so to speak), was the need for a dubbing of wool from a ram's testicles. This was mixed with seal's fur and hair from the head of a hare. Not only the first, but all three are materials I might find difficult to obtain by hand, hence my reason for favouring the shop-bought variety.

I had started my fishing on Tweed tributaries, the Lyne Water and

A Tweed grayling

the Manor above Peebles, but eventually graduated to the hallowed pools of the main river. This was when I first met grown-up anglers, men who had fished the Tweed for years and knew the water well. They taught me to read the river and to use my eyes to see what the fish were feeding on. I now had waders rather than wellies, and with slightly more sophisticated tackle, I could cover the water better and was gaining that unpurchasable commodity, experience. And so it was on Holylee, a delightful stretch of water, that I took my first ever trout of that magic weight, a pound. I still remember the thud as the fish took and the thrill when the spring balance registered that the fish was a pound and an ounce and a wee bit. Dream Number One realised.

But it is a fact of life, is it not, that that which once seemed unattainable, once attained, subsequently may seem mundane. After that first pounder-plus came to the net, others followed, and again the Tweed was the fruitful source. 'More matter for a May morning,' says Fabian in Shakespeare's *Twelfth Night* (a part I played at the Lyceum Theatre in Edinburgh many years later), proved to be a brown trout of 4 pounds 10 ounces from Yair while fishing for early-summer salmon. According to the scale reading, it was a hen fish deteriorating in condition which had four salmon parr and a water vole in its stomach. To this date, it remains the second-heaviest wild brown trout I've ever taken, beaten only by that 6-pounder from Loch Assynt in Sutherland. I'm no perfectionist, but I have to say that I value the Tweed fish more highly as it was taken on fly.

These Tweed men also spoke of salmon and sea trout and grayling. We fished the lower Tweed with Mike Maule, that enthusiastic English-Scottish coarse fisher, and took grayling up to 2 pounds. *Thymallus thymallus* is, like the canary in the coal-mine, an indicator of quality. Find their shoals and you know the river is in good condition, as they cannot survive in polluted water. Fishing light tackle and small baits, there is double delight to be had in the sport they give in winter and the knowledge that the river is in good health.

The Tweed men made me aware, too, of a world downstream near St Boswells, Kelso and Coldstream where some of the finest salmon fishing in Scotland was to be had. Out came the books, and I read for the first time about Bemersyde, Mertoun, Rutherford, Makerstoun, Floors, the Junction, Hendersyde, Birgham, Carham, Wark and down to the Lees at Coldstream. So, as I grew into a more experienced angler, salmon vied with trout for fishing thrills, and thoughts of that 20-pounder loomed large.

With the Duke of Roxburghe on Upper Floors

Over the years I managed to sneak the odd day on one or two of the better beats, but it was not easy fishing to get or to afford: pocket-money was not sufficient to furnish fishing on Floors. But when it was decided to centre our lower Tweed programme on Kelso, it seemed natural to feature fishing on some of these famous beats, to share Floors, the Junction and the Lees with our viewers.

Sir Guy David Innes Ker – tenth Duke of Roxburghe, eleventh Baronet, a Chieftain of Clan Ker – and his family live in Floors Castle, just outside Kelso. If ever there was the perfect setting for a grand home, surely this is it. Overlooking the Tweed, with a background of the rolling Cheviot Hills where much of the Roxburghe lands are found, this family seat was designed and built by William Adam between 1718 and 1740 to the desires of John Ker, fifth Earl of Roxburghe. He had been Secretary of State for Scotland and his efforts to smooth the passage of the Act of Union in 1707 had been rewarded by Queen Anne by the granting of a dukedom, and he wished for a grand house to reflect his elevation to first Duke of Roxburghe. About a hundred years later, the sixth Duke called in the noted architect William Playfair to add embellishment, altering the house to its present appearance. The castle is open to the public nowadays and the visitor will be impressed by the rare tapestries, fine antiques, paintings by masters and priceless Chinese porcelain, all exhibited in the castle's beautifully preserved period rooms. In the basement are many interesting items, including a basket woven by Queen Victoria, a letter written by Mary, Queen of Scots on 25 September 1566, a collection of guns, including a 4-bore fowling piece with a 4-foot 6-inch barrel, and, of course, there is a fishing-room with antique tackle: reels, rods and some fascinating ancient salmon flies.

In a glass case is a salmon of 57½ pounds, reputed to be one of the largest caught on rod and line from the Tweed. It was taken in 1886 by a Mr Arthur Pryor on the Floors Water, and his account makes fascinating reading. He had a good day's sport, taking 14 fish up to 30 pounds by four o'clock before he hooked the monster. Now, I'd have been more than happy with half that number up to half that weight, but in those days there were some prodigious catches made. Mr Pryor then hooked what he felt to be 'a heavy fish, which took all my strength to hold him. After trying all he knew to get rid of the hook he went down through the rocks in safety. I then had hold of him for half an hour and my arms ached painfully'. I'm not surprised. Mr Pryor was probably fishing a cane or greenheart rod of up to 18 feet – no lightweight to wield and a devil with which to play a heavy fish. 'Downstream went the fish again but after an hour's hard struggle, floated tail first into the landing net.' I would happily have suffered several rigorous hours for the prize of a fish over 50 pounds, as I was still a pound and a half short of my goal, and that after 30 years of fishing.

The two Floors beats, upper and lower, are famous for their salmon fishing, and surely one of the great benefits of owning fishing rights to a piece of water is that you can decide and promulgate the rules. Normally, salmon beats are let for the six fishing days in the week – by law there is no fishing for salmon on a Sunday – but His Grace keeps Saturdays on upper Floors for himself and his guests. He is such a keen fisher, he reckons that if he didn't let the other days, he'd be tempted to slip down for a cast or two every day. His father was also a dedicated fisher, taking the family to sample the big fish delights of salmon fishing in Norway every summer. It was there that Sir Guy took his heaviest, a 51-pounder, and two 47-pounders on consecutive nights, though he started as a lad trout fishing aged five or six and took his first salmon from Upper Floors on a 9-foot rod, fishing for trout. This is perhaps one of the Tweed's three most famous and prolific beats, but when we spoke, the water was unseasonably low and, though there were fish in the Floors pools, even His Grace had to be content with a well-conditioned trout of about three-quarters of a pound – which, with a neat irony reflecting his first salmon, was taken on a 16-foot fly-rod.

Many of the famous middle and lower Tweed beats are let to the same anglers year after year and it is difficult and expensive to become part of that scene. But through the initiative of James Leeming and his self-devised computerised booking system, it is possible to fish some of the most prestigious beats in summer for only a modest outlay. All you need to do is to turn up at one of the Borders tackle shops where there is a computer terminal, pick from what is available, pay your dues and high-tail it to the river. From around £25 per day, you can cast a fly on Bemersyde and Ladykirk, Pedwell and West Learmouth and Junction, Sprouston and the Lees, and if you hit the water with summer rain and in good condition, your chances of getting fish are high.

The Lees is classic water, with the famous Temple Pool one of the most productive on the whole river. Over 500 yards long, this and the Cauld Pool in autumn offer the chance for red-letter catches. The Lees' proprietor, Andrew Douglas-Home, explained that here, on the lower lower Tweed, where the river forms the border between Scotland and

England, any legal problems that might have arisen through the fact that laws are different in the two countries, have been addressed by an Act of Parliament dating back to the 1850s. The river is administered by the Tweed Commissioners, who also employ a bailiff force to police the river.

The Tweed has always been a target for professional gangs of poachers, some recently coming from as far away as Wales. In 1993 the Tweed Commissioners made arrests involving gangs from Dumfries, Northumberland and Dalkeith. Illegal nets were placed at many points on the lower river and beaches and the gangs moved in and out quickly. There were instances of poachers wearing camouflage wet-suits sweeping through holding pools and taking large numbers of fish. In one incident, after a gang was disturbed, 60 salmon were recovered. In the same year, 528 nets were found, 140 more than the previous year, although the number of fish taken illegally was down. There seemed to be a hard core of habitual poachers, known to the commissioners, and that battle is beginning to be won. As is that against the foul-hooking brigade throughout the system. Those who continue to perpetrate illegal rod fishing – mainly on Association water – by the foul-hooking of salmon at the back end of the season, have been sussed. Their permits have been withdrawn and there is also a blacklist of those who may be tempted to join the band of brigands for whom it matters not how the fish come out of the water, whether hooked in mouth, back or tail. I fear the commissioners will never be without work.

Andrew kindly arranged for me to cast a fly on the Lees, and, with ghillie Malcolm Campbell at the oars, we eased across the gap at the Cauld Pool on a crisp autumn morning, our hopes high. I had decided to fish my old favourite 14-foot spliced Sharp's Impregnated fly rod with a Hardy Perfect reel and on Malcolm's advice I coupled it with a slow sinker and 2-inch Black Shrimp tube fly. It was popply water, about 39 degrees – cold enough to make the fish think twice about running the Cauld – but fish were showing. A head and tail here and there, 'cogging' we used to call it in the old days. It was only minutes before a slow draw was converted into a lively fish. In the net, it had sea-lice . . . well, one sea-louse – indicating its recent journey from salt to fresh water. Glinting silver in the late-autumn sun, it was the epitome of all a salmon angler could wish for at the end of October.

A few more casts and a heavier fish took hold and it was a delight to see the old cane rod arc as the fish ran down the pool. Fifteen minutes later Malcolm slipped the net under a fish of 17½ pounds. It was slightly

Billy the ghillie reckons it's over 20 pounds!

damaged about the fins, but was the heaviest I had ever caught on the fly. Still not that elusive 20-pounder, though.

And so to the Junction. Jim Miller, who fishes there late season, had invited us to where Teviot meets Tweed at Kelso, on perhaps the most famous of all the lower Tweed salmon beats. He also has Tay fishing which closes on 15 October, and, as the Tweed fishes to the end of November, he invites his Tay ghillies for a day or two of friendly rivalry. I was acting ghillie for Dave Seaton as he played, and I landed for him, a bright hen fish. Like the Duke, Mr Miller has house rules, and all hen fish and coloured cocks are returned to the water. I hand-tailed Dave's fish for him and it was slipped back to the river. Asking how I rated in the ghillie-ing stakes, Dave suggested that I had done well, but might have been a mite quicker. Nine out of ten were the points he awarded me.

Now, I had saved hard to put a fly over this hallowed water a few times over the years and had taken a fish or two, but never at the back end of the season when, if ever it is possible to guarantee a fish, this has to be the place. Mr Miller said he was going for a haircut the following morning and offered us the boat below Kelso Bridge until he was tonso-

72

That 20-pounder

rially satisfied – perhaps a couple of hours. We met at the fishing lodge and got our gear together, and I was trembling again as Billy the ghillie rowed me out to the neck of the run. There are rocky ledges here, with up to 30 feet of water providing resting-places for many fish. Once again the water was low, and though I'd have liked a better flow to make the fly work naturally, Billy told me to cast at 45 degrees, let the fly sink, allow the river to bring the fly into the deep channel and then hand-line slowly back to the boat. I'm never quite sure what to do if a fish takes when hand-lining, but Billy's advice was simple. Just keep pulling and it will be on.

Ten minutes later, I did just that and it was on. Then it was off. The fish shot off downstream at a rate of knots and threw the hook. Billy suggested a change of angle and fly. Both were achieved and a few minutes later, as I was drawing the fly upstream, I felt a magical thump and was into another salmon. This one stayed on; as it came to the surface for the first time, Billy reckoned it to be a good fish, perhaps 20-plus. Well, if I wasn't nervous enough about landing it before, now I was a ball of lard. Luck was on my side this time, though, and after what seemed an eternity, Billy netted what I thought a big fish – a hen fish – and as such, a fish to be returned. The hook was gently removed and I asked the 30-year question. 'What weight would you give it, Billy?'

'Twenty-plus' were his magical words. This from a chap who has landed many heavy fish in the line of duty. Who was I to argue? The fish was put back in the river and made off, leaving a wake that would have done credit to a Channel hovercraft.

My knees were jelly, I could barely speak and I was dimly aware that the Tweed had yet again made dreams come true. Or had it? There was no tangible evidence. The spring balance had not thudded down to over 20 pounds and it was only Billy's educated word (which, I may say, I did not doubt) that allowed elation to spring from my breast. And I rather like it that way. I'll never know its *exact* weight, but I do know that fish was the biggest I've ever caught and that will do me nicely, especially as it was caught on the fly.

As we got back into the boat, Mr Miller came up the riverbank and asked how we'd done. It was difficult not to be boring and I succumbed. He listened with interest and I can never thank him enough for providing me with the chance to realise that second boyhood dream. And I'm glad both were realised on that wonderful river, the Tweed, which, as I am sure you will realise, now holds a very special place in my heart.

Chapter 8

WESTER ROSS

Mystical Maree

Somehow the name doesn't quite do justice to the setting. From the viewpoint on the Achnasheen to Kinlochewe road, you look down the valley towards Loch Maree. It is a gateway to some of the most beautiful scenery in Scotland – Wester Ross, stretching from the River Kirkaig in the north to Lochcarron in the south by way of Achiltibuie, Ullapool, Gairloch and Torridon – and you are looking towards all that beauty down Glen Docherty. It should be in Gaelic and mean something like 'the Green Glen with the beautiful view towards Loch Maree'. I'm afraid I haven't the Gaelic, but I'm sure that doesn't translate as Glen Docherty.

No matter, the view is superb and we headed down the glen, turning left at Kinlochewe to meet Iain Fraser, former policeman and manager of Torridon House Hotel at the time. We had a cup of tea and a blether, then out came the hotel's fishing book. It is always fascinating to look through the records of years past and to see how present catches compare. Sadly, like so many other places in Scotland, the sea trout fishing has deteriorated greatly in recent years. When conditions are right, though, the book showed people still caught salmon and brown trout. One entry read: 'Snow, rain, drizzle, cloudy, tempest, hurricane and balmy – typical Torridon weather.' But I'm not so sure. When was it ever balmy?

It was raining even as we read the book, so the teacups were emptied and fishing gear donned. We headed for the loch at the top of the Torridon River. Loch-an-Iasgaich, the 'loch of the fish' in translation. Small, with reedy fringes, it holds decent numbers of salmon when there is sufficient water for the fish to run. Iain said they congregate where the burn from the hills enters the loch and at the edge of the reeds. The reeds are best fished from the boat and it can be thrilling to see a neb and dorsal porpoise at the fly as the fish comes out of its reedy cover. At the incoming burn mouth, there was a convenient spit of land from which to cast into likely water. Stealth is all when a fish might be lying at the edge of the current in shallow water, just waiting to make the next step of the journey upstream.

Conditions were fine – for once no excuse there – my senses were sharp and, as I made the first casts, every nerve, ganglion and synapse was crackling with electrical expectancy. Some time later, there had been a distinct drain on the batteries. I had moved nothing, rested the water, moved nothing again, rested the water again, been what I imagine an object of mirth to a small brown frog as it made its way up the 'frog and toad' for the night, and an object of derision to myself as I managed to outwit only the tiniest sea trout. The answer had to be local knowledge. Iain. He tied on a wee silver butcher and had a cast or two over the same water. I thought it only fair to give his optimism free rein before we returned to the hotel – when, he simply said, 'There we are, Paul.' Chilling, chilling words indeed. Iain had hooked a fish. It was in the net a few minutes later – under arrest and detained for questioning. There were certainly questions I would like to have asked. Why did it take the butcher and not the whatever-I-was-using? But, as I've said before, until a salmon can speak we'll never know. The fish was typical of those taken in the Highlands in summer. Marked on the belly through negotiating a stony and boulder-strewn river, a trifle coloured, but game to the last. As we packed up in the falling dusk, the midges dictated a fast retreat to the hotel bar to discuss why Glen Docherty wasn't called something else. Well, I was ready to talk about anything but the fishing.

I love the way Country and Western songs tell a story. I am thinking of writing one about this part of Scotland. This new style, I'll call 'Country and Wester-Rossian'.

The mist lifts from Loch Maree

When in the North, good fishing you search,
Take a rod or a pole; you may catch a perch,
Wester Ross has 'most any fish that you like,
In a wee loch by the road, if the weather is right,
You may get a surprise, in the shape of a pike!

Sing this to the tune of 'Drop-kick me, Jesus, through the Goal-Posts of Life' and it'll be next stop Nashville.

We wandered down from the road to the little loch which we had been told was one of the most north-westerly on the mainland holding perch and pike. The float settled nicely, the worm dangling enticingly below. The anticipation of that first wibble-wobble of the float, indicating some interest from under the surface, is a delightful agony, which takes me back to boyhood days. Perch were the quarry then, too, and part of their charm lay in their willingness to take what must have been a crudely presented bait. Pugnacious and cheeky, with crimson fins and a spiny dorsal that seems to say 'Wha daur meddle wi' me', perch have diminished in number in Scottish waters over the years, with disease reckoned to be the culprit; happily, though, they now seem to be at least holding their own.

My reverie was interrupted by the float's movement – a gentle bob, a pause, another wiggle and then it slipped under the surface. It was a perch, and as I brought it to shore, memories came flooding back. If ever one needed to be reminded that fishing is not just about catching big fish, here was the moment. The sight and smell of that wee perch took me instantly back to Duddingston Loch well over 30 years ago: transport there was a Royal Enfield bike with Sturmey-Archer three-speed gear and dynamo for the lights which, when applied to the wheel, made the bike harder to pedal; green solid glass rod with Intrepid reel and Platil nylon, or was it Kroik?; and we'll be talking next about Mucilin and Colorado Spoons and Young's of Redditch and their Condex reels – all of these fleeting glimpses of my angling past brought to mind again by the sight of this one little fish. I returned it to the water as carefully as possible, thankful for the memories it had jogged.

Sheep wandered past, following each other like, well, sheep; birds filled the air with music, and perch after perch took the float under. A splendid session, with a small pike taken on a worm providing an interesting coda. That there was just the right amount of breeze to keep the midges quiet added to the pleasure. It may seem odd to have been in pursuit of coarse fish in an excellent game fishing area, but I loved it.

Next morning, we took to the sands to dig some bait for a day's seafishing. There are always places in Wester Ross where you can dig a lugworm or two, and, as we headed for the shore, we became aware of what looked like a crescent-shaped wall, an arc of stones built from the Ploc of Torridon, over the sand to the north shore of Upper Loch Torridon at Fasag. We met Donnie London. (He's known as Donnie London because he worked there and also so that he is not confused with another Donnie, Donnie Merchant, who is one.) It seems the stones were built where they are for a purpose: to trap fish. Donnie explained that the wall was built low at the north end and high at the south. It seems fish always came into the bay on the north side as the tide flooded and the low wall allowed them into the trap, but when the tide dropped, the water escaped between the stones at the high end and left the fish stranded as they tried to get out of the bay on the south side. Cunning. After the trap had been built for a few years, mussels would grow on it and hold the stones together so that winter waves wouldn't destroy it, but still let the water out and leave the fish. Even more cunning. It was a very effective trap for salmon, sea trout, herring and mackerel – any fish, in fact, that came close inshore in search of spawning burns or food. A high tide about two o'clock in the morning was ideal, especially on a

78

dark night with mist and drizzle and Donnie remembers sitting on the rock at the top of the wall waiting to see what was in the trap. But woe betide him if he had shone the torch before the wall had cleared the water, as the fish might have seen the top and gone over. It was a sophisticated device in that the stones at the highest point were removable, allowing any fish which were not required to escape. The Gaelic name for the trap is a *carraigh*. I kept forgetting the name and Ricky Walker suggested I used *Cary* Grant as an *aide-mémoire*. It should have been all right, but for some reason, I then kept referring to the trap as a Gregory.

The wealth of fishing for the trout angler in Wester Ross takes in wonderful waters like Sionascaig in the shadows of Stac Polly, Cul Mor and Cul Beag, Lochs Oscaig, Bad a' Ghaill and Lurgainn at the foot of Ben More Coigach, Fionn Loch in the Letterewe Forest to the north of Loch Maree and Loch Damph emptying into Upper Loch Torridon under the road to Shieldaig at the Falls of Balgy. All of these waters produce prodigious numbers of trout every year and can give excellent sport for those just visiting for the day. In addition, there are many smaller waters where fishing can be had for a modest outlay and where any angler may make a good catch of that most precious commodity, wild Scottish brown trout. For those with a modicum of wanderlust, there are lochs in the hills that are seldom fished and which repay the effort made to reach them with the knowledge that the fish have been well earned.

And take a day away without the rods. Visit Applecross via the exhilarating Bealach na Bo (The Pass of the Cattle) and find one of the earliest seats of Christianity in Scotland, where the followers of St Maelrubha are buried in the old churchyard. This is a collection of small villages with wonderful names: Camusterrach, Camustiel, Toscaig and Culduie. Or explore the Beinn Eighe Nature Reserve, the first in Britain, where, with Beinn Alligin and Liathach, you may see red and roe deer, pine marten and wildcat, ptarmigan and golden eagle. Wander round the sub-tropical Inverewe Garden, giving a wonderful display of colour throughout the year. Take a walk onto the suspension bridge at Corrieshalloch Gorge and watch the Falls of Measach tumble 150 feet into the mile-long gorge. Those who, like me, suffer from vertigo, will be happy to hear others tell of the magnificent sight. Near Aultbea, follow the Naval History Trail at Mellon Charles and take the shoes off and have a paddle on the sandy beach at Mellon Udrigle. Go shopping in Ullapool, now gateway to Stornoway and the Outer Hebrides. Planned and built by the British Fisheries Society in 1788, it was the herring capital of the north-west. Now, you can see the Klondykers from Eastern Europe in Loch Broom, buying vast numbers of mackerel. Go to Achiltibuie and visit the Smokehouse and Hydroponicum set up by Robert Irvine. Follow 'the wee mad road' towards Lochinver and Sutherland and visit the desolate and beautiful Inverpolly Nature Reserve, a home to many rare animals and plants. There is no shortage of things to see and do here in Wester Ross, one of Europe's finest wildernesses.

Back to the fishing. All was calm at Gairloch, where visitors were happily spending an hour or two on the pier. A husband and wife, plus dog, remembered catches of haddock ten years previously. A Dutch boy, spinning for mackerel, caught a jellyfish, one of those blueish jobs that turn up in their thousands each summer. Couldn't lift it up onto the pier, though. A man from the Isle of Man was catching mackerel and giving them to people to take home, complete with instructions on how to cook them. There was a wonderfully relaxed atmosphere as people simply enjoyed being there – just what holidays in Wester Ross are all about. Even the seagulls looked fairly relaxed as we all prepared for the following day's exploits, a trip aboard the *Kerry* to explore some marks in Outer Loch Torridon where, scallop-divers had told us, there were skate and rays in goodly numbers.

With skipper Sandy MacKenzie, we first of all had to get bait. The mackerel were co-operative and it was not long before we were off Red Point at the outer end of Loch Torridon. Several species of flatfish taken out from Gairloch have figured in the Scottish record list, the dab of 2¾ pounds and the cuckoo ray of 5¼ being just a couple. The mark we were on was known to be a place where thornback rays had been taken, and with the Scottish record standing at just a touch under 30 pounds, tackle had to be carefully chosen. I was fishing 15-pound nylon with a short wire trace and a slice of fresh mackerel. The bites are not shy when they come and Sandy had picked the spot well, the rod tip soon nodding as a fish took off with what it thought was a free meal. No such thing as a free lunch, they say, and soon a hard-fighting thornback was netted by Sandy. As the name implies, these fish have prickles or spines along the back and tail, so thick rubber gloves are recommended when unhooking thornbacks. There seemed to be a fair old pack below us, well-conditioned fish around the 10 to 12-pound mark. Thornback wings make good eating, the traditional way being to serve them with a black butter sauce. Having no butter of any colour with us, we returned our fish to the water, then

A thornback – gloved hands essential

went back to Gairloch after an exhilarating day afloat.

From sea to Maree. Many people who know the beauties of Scotland put Loch Maree high on the list, some hailing it as the most beautiful in the country. Set between Slioch and the Letterewe Forest to the north-east and Kinlochewe Forest and Beinn Eighe to the south-west, it has brown trout, char and salmon but is most famous for the quality of its sea trout fishing, some huge fish being taken every year. After the recent fall in catches of this favourite sporting fish, happily there are signs that numbers are improving again.

Traditionally, Maree is a loch for the dapper. No, you don't have to wear a smart suit; the trees on the shore might be spruce but the angler can dress casual. Dapping is the method of fishing with a long rod, floss silk line and letting the breeze tumble and dance the fly on the wave. It is a thrilling way to cover the water as the angler sees every fish that comes to the fly, but it is not for the faint-hearted. Head keeper Frank Buckley fishes a 6 to 8-foot cast and recommends that you do not tighten until the floss hits the water. Old boatmen speak of seeing the fish take the fly, then filling and lighting their pipe, *then* tightening into the fish. Whichever way you want to deal with a rise to the dap, it takes a steely nerve.

The loch is divided into numerous beats and boats out from Loch Maree Hotel have the chance to explore some wonderful water round the many islands where the Scots pines still stand tall and proud – a picturesque reminder of how this part of Scotland must have looked before so much native timber was taken for charcoal to fill the fiery maws of the early iron foundries. The history of the islands can be traced back to the seventh century when St Maelrubha, the Celtic missionary and he of the Applecross followers, founded a monastic cell on Isle Maree. The Vikings used the loch as a raiding base, bringing their boats into Loch Ewe and either up the River Ewe or dragging them overland. There are Viking and Christian reminders on Isle Maree, oak and holly as well as pine – and the wishing tree. Frank told me that this is a legacy of what began as a pagan ritual but developed into a Christian one. When St Maelrubha blessed people or cured the sick, they would leave a gift of thanks, clothing or a coin, the former hung from the tree, the latter wedged into the bark.

Isle Maree has an atmosphere about it that is difficult to describe. There is a superstition that anyone removing anything from the island will suffer ill-fortune. The old ghillies even went so far as to make sure

Evening on Loch Maree

that, after lunching on the shore, there was not a stone, pebble or even a speck of Isle Maree sand on their boots or clothing before they got back into the boat. I was happy to leave a coin of thanks in the tree, and also made sure my boots and clothes carried nothing from this truly enchanted place.

Back out on the loch, Frank and I were suffering from a lack of wind. No hard-boiled eggs in the packed-lunches perhaps, but it did make fishing difficult. Frank suggested a trip to a loch on one of the islands. I liked the idea of fishing a loch on an island in a loch, but the hike through the heather made me think that whoever penned the song 'Marching through the Heather' had never done it. It is difficult enough to walk through, far less march. How Neville did it with a camera at his shoulder, I know not. He deserves a Duke of Edinburgh Award.

We got there on an evening of rare beauty. The sun was low in the sky, and as we breasted the rise the lochan lay before us. Not a breath of wind ruffled its surface, trout were rising and all was ear-shatteringly quiet; it was stunningly beautiful. Yet Scotland, being the country it is, doesn't give up its treasures easily. The midges were out. In force. Flights of them, commanded, it seemed, by crack pilots. They homed in on us, standing targets. Neville and I looked at each other and, being strong and decisive men, came to an instant decision. We ran for it, got into the boat, shot back to Loch Maree Hotel and shared the calamine lotion, which, as the old song says, is so good for the skin.

Maybe Neville or I did unknowingly take just a speck of sand from Isle Maree and the spirits thought we should be reminded that Wester Ross, Loch Maree and Isle Maree *are* special places. If that was the case, we apologise, and are grateful to the spirits for letting us off easy. A few midge bites are a small price to pay for allowing us familiarity with one of the most magnificent places on earth.

Chapter 9

ORKNEY

Islands of Plenty

I really know I'm back in Orkney when I walk down the streets of Kirkwall and see the names above the shops. Certainly, here are ubiquitous and nationwide establishments like building societies, banks and department stores, but the names I love are Rendall, Tough, Glue, Flett and Isbister – real Orcadian sounds. And signposts pointing to places like Quoys, Quanterness, Quholm and Quoyloo. Leaving the queues, say Heddle and Twatt and Settiscarth and Hobbister and you have to be in Orkney. And it is not just the names that are redolent of these northern isles. Stop for a chat or to ask directions and enjoy the accents, unlike those of the north of Scotland, and with their distinctive lilt of Scandinavian, you are reminded of the history of Orkney.

First described around 330 BC by the Greek explorer Pytheas and mentioned by Tacitus after the Battle of Mons Graupius in AD 49, the most influential incomers were the Vikings from about the eighth century onwards, and still today, most Orkney place-names come from Old Norse. St Magnus Cathedral, the building of which was started in 1137, was a tribute by Earl Rognvald to the memory of his Uncle Magnus, and despite the many other Viking remains on the islands, it is the grandest by far.

There are over 70 islands and skerries, about 20 of which are permanently inhabited. Lying on the same latitude as the southern tip of Greenland, Orkney's climate is suprisingly equable, mild with little snow or frost. The sea exerts its influence, however, and the islands have been known to have a wet and windy day or two. The land is fairly rich, farming being the main industry, with beef cattle, dairy farming and a variety of crops.

And then there's the water. Orkney's clean, cold salt water is great for lobster, crab and scallop. I well remember one of the best meals of my life. We were sea fishing out from Stromness and had a basket or two of scallops on board. It was cold and there was a decent swell running as we fished whole squid baits for ling over rocky gullies off the cliffs at St John's Head. The boat was rolling comprehensively and the last thing on our minds, you might have thought, would be food. But the skipper threw some scallops into a pan of sea-water, brought it to the boil and emptied them into the sink. We ate these wonderful, creamy, sweet, fishy bites accompanied by draughts of Orkney malt and cans of beer, all soaked up with chunks of thick, white Stromness bread. No, we didn't stop fishing, because we were getting big ling regularly; we reached in through the open window of the galley and helped ourselves as the mood took. With snow flurries, a cutting wind and the boat rolling like a roller-coaster, it was not easy, but we managed to empty those couple of baskets.

And Orkney is rich in fresh water, too. The wild brown trout fishing in the lochs of Pomona or Mainland is in a class of its own. There are six main lochs, and many smaller, all accessible to the visiting angler. The old Norse Udal law still pertains (*Udal* meaning without feudal superior) and technically all fishing is free. It would be churlish, however, not to contribute to the excellent work done by the enthusiasts forming the Orkney Trout Fishing Association who work hard to maintain the excellence of the fishing. They make an annual stocking of waters under their control and all they ask is that you join for the duration of your stay, which I reckon is a small price to pay for access to so much great trout fishing. The six main waters are Loch of Harray, which is joined to Loch of Stenness, Loch of Boardhouse, Loch of Swannay, Loch of Hundland and Loch of Kirbister. There are other, smaller waters, such as Loch of Clumly, Loch of Sabiston and Loch of Isbister.

Stan Headley, being an Orcadian and a dedicated trout fisher, knows these waters well and suggested we try Loch of Harray, the largest and most popular loch. Boats are available at various points round the shoreline, though wading can be successful. And that intimate knowlege is important. To look at Harray and compare it with many Scottish mainland lochs, one might imagine that once away from the shore, you can open the throttle of the outboard and aim where you please. Not so. One of the reasons for Harray's fertility is the fact that many parts are shallow – so shallow that the skerries reach to just below the surface all over the loch. Many a visitor, and I guess some Orcadians, will have encountered these outboard-destroying rocks at high speed. It is little wonder that you are always advised to take replacement shear-pins with you when afloat. But these self-same skerries are where the trout are lurking. The water is shallow round them, and the light produces good feeding. The trout graze the algae from the skerry stones and feed on pea mussels and other molluscs. There is deep water close at hand, so the fish feel safe. Each skerry, and there are many on Harray, is a micro-environment in which a variety of creatures, including the trout, thrive.

A pint on the lawn of the Merkister Hotel, with owner Angus MacDonald

But even before skerry-awareness, one has to become Orkney-fly smart. I opened my fly boxes to Stan's critical eye and they were pronounced a southern collection. Unsurprising, as that's where I fish most. Stan's flies were different. Bigger, brasher and braver was how he described them. More flash, more colour and, unlike myself, with more hair. Flies for the top dropper, to be tickled through the wave and bring fish to the surface. That does not mean that the flies were coarsely tied. Stan takes care at the vice; his flies may be larger than those for southern waters, but they are all beautifully tied. Bumbles of infinite variety, selections of palmered fancies and attractors tied with all the variety that new materials can offer. My box looked like an antique alongside Stan's modern and personal fishing statement. And he can tie flies for the south, too – witness the fact that he won the National Championship fished on Loch Leven, a completely different style of fishing from his native Orkney lochs.

So, out we went on Harray, and although we had less than perfect conditions, with more north in the wind than we would have liked, Stan managed to find a drift or two where the fish were willing to come to both selections of flies. And these fish are a reminder of what a wonderful natural asset we have in our wild brown trout. Not always heavyweights, but that doesn't matter. They rise freely to the fly, sometimes missing spectacularly, but they may come a second and even third time if you can get the fly back on the water quickly enough. And the visual enjoyment of seeing them come to the surface is what trout anglers enjoy most. A

Billy Sinclair's Swannay trout

floating line, I reckon, and hairy flies which bring fish to the surface sure beats having to fish deep just to catch fish. And Orkney is a place where anglers come back year after year to enjoy that pleasure. They are seldom disappointed.

I also fished Loch of Swannay with Billy Sinclair from Stromness. The shoreline stones, when lifted, were alive with shrimp. These Orkney fish are well fed, hence their wonderful condition. Again the shallows were productive and fish to about a pound and a half fell for the bulkier flies. Swannay is a peatier loch than Harray and the trout are darker as a result, but no less handsome. Though peaty, Swannay produces big fish every season; 3-pounders are not uncommon and fish to 6 pounds are no rarity. Class wild brown trout.

And for an area with little running fresh water, Orkney can provide some surprisingly good sea trout fishing. We fished along the shoreline with Stan Headley, marvelling at the economical and efficient way he explored likely taking places. This tends to be the kind of fishing for the solitary angler; one who knows the water at all stages of the tide, and who can capitalise on that knowledge by fishing quickly, quietly and cleanly for these elusive and shy fish. They feed in the seaweed, sometimes very close to shore, and are to be taken on fly and a variety of baits. Sandeel and worm have proved their worth. But you have to cover a lot of water and it is perhaps best not to be encumbered with fishing pals – just one rod quartering likely water while the tide and conditions are right.

One Sunday evening we went for a look at a likely spot for filming and things were just right. The water was clear and we saw fish moving but, being a Sunday, we did not fish. During the night the wind got up and next morning saw the bottom stirred up, the wind blowing straight into our faces and fishing conditions rendered useless. These are the vicissitudes that befall any angler, whether or not a film unit is waiting in the background, and we caught no sea trout that day.

There is one place, however, where sea trout are to be found regularly. I say found, not caught. Loch of Stenness, joined to Loch of Harray between the Ring of Brodgar and the Stones of Stenness, is a brackish loch. Tides bring an influx of salt water and fish from the Hoy Sound through the Bay of Ireland and by way of the Bush to the loch. Stenness is rich in mixed feeding: shrimp, snail and flies common in fresh water as well as crab and flies lurking in the seaweed. It is little wonder that Orkney's heaviest trout of 29 pounds was taken from here, but perhaps a more surprising catch was a turbot of over 18 pounds. Scope here, perhaps, for a new British record fly-caught flattie. But Stenness does not give up its fish easily. Rich natural feeding means artificial flies are often of secondary consideration to the fish. Wading is not always easy because of mud, boulders and weed, but it pays to persevere. Large brown and sea trout are taken every year and they are fish to be treasured. We came across Iain Hutcheson on a dreich evening, but for him it was a great night. He had a lovely brown trout and a split fresh sea trout of about 4 pounds, the sea-lice testifying to the fact that it was not long from undiluted salt water. For those with that extra bit of commitment, Stenness can reward their staying-power handsomely.

The historical side of Orkney meets you at every turn. If you stand on the narrow road between Harray and Stenness, as anglers do, just looking at the water and cogitating about the day ahead, the Ring of Brodgar and the Standing Stones of Stenness are further evidence of man's hand extending back many thousands of years. The Ring of Brodgar, reckoned to be one of the finest stone circles anywhere, has 27 of the original 60 stones still standing. Excavation dates it to sometime in the third millennium BC, a similar age being attributed to the Stones at Stenness. These were dated from finds of pottery, animal bones and, slightly scarily, a human finger. Whose was it, and how did it get there? An ancient fisherman digging for worms?

I first stood in the middle of the Ring of Brodgar one November afternoon, with the wind whistling through the stones. The clouds were racing across the sky and, just occasionally, shafts of watery sunlight speared down on the surrounding land. The hills of Hoy were momentarily lit dramatically and just as quickly lost in the cloud. It was eerie but uplifting and I felt a great sense of the history of these wonderful works built by people long gone. A testament to their beliefs and humbling in their seeming simplicity.

There are more modern reminders of Orkney's history, too. The Churchill Barriers were built between the Mainland, Lamb Holm, Glimps Holm, Burray and South Ronaldsay as a defence against the threat of German submarines from the east, and the Italian Chapel on Lamb Holm, 'The Miracle of Camp 60', where in 1943 Domenico Chiocchetti and other Italian prisoners-of-war, who helped build the Barriers, also created an ornate Chapel out of two Nissen huts. In 1960 Mr Chiocchetti returned to restore the paintwork and the Chapel is now one of the most visited monuments in Orkney. Mr Chiocchetti told the people of Orkney that the Chapel is theirs 'to love and preserve'. Fitting

that the two countries, at war so long ago, now have a point of contact for   *Hoxa Head pollack*
ever.

    And as we moved south over the Barriers, happily these days providing a link between the islands rather than a defence against incomers (and, it has to be said, some excellent fishing), it was time to try for the pollack off Hoxa Head. There are times in winter when the weather and tides in the Sound of Hoxa between South Ronaldsay and Flotta are just right, so it was a wan early-December sun that greeted us as we carefully descended the cliffs to a table of rock that let us cast into deep water.

    You have got to be careful in situations like this; rogue waves can test even the most wary of anglers but I felt I was in good company fishing with Malcolm Russell, Orkney Mainland's only safety officer and a keen sea angler. At this time of year, daylight is in short supply, so you have to make the most of it. I had brought an ordinary salmon spinning reel, but when I hooked my first fish I wished I'd heeded the advice to use a large capacity spool. These pollack dive fast for the kelp, and you need to get line on the reel as fast as possible to keep the fish coming up. I lost several, but landed some. They weren't big, but fish here can go to double figures, so it doesn't pay to be mimsy. Fish sensibly for what you might catch and you'll find it easier to land and return those hard-fighting pollack.

Deep-sea fishing in Orkney waters is well known. Halibut have been taken, and skate, ling and shark. Many years ago, I remember looking into a deep-freeze on Stromness Pier with ex-Provost Bunt Knight. The object of our admiration lay within and was Bunt's new British record halibut of 163 pounds, a fish taken at the edge of a tide race on an evening jaunt for haddock – surprise, surprise. It was one of the biggest fish I had ever seen, a mighty fish, and the halibut is still a species that makes anglers tremble at the thought of hooking one. Smaller species like pollack, coalfish and codling are taken from boats on the drift off the west side of Hoy from St John's Head south past Rackwick Bay to Tor Ness and off some of the skerries out in the Pentland Firth, assuming the tide is in a benign state.

There is fishing to be explored all over – the Northern Isles, flatties from the many sandy bays and, of course, those sea trout. Coupled with this is a wonderful diversity of plant- and animal-life. For the bird-watcher, there are RSPB reserves on Orkney Mainland, Hoy, Rousay and Westray amongst others, and the variety of habitat within a relatively small area encourages a huge divergence of species – over 300 counted and over 100 breeding on the isles. Plant-life, too, reflects Orkney's richness of habitats. Orchids and the rare Scottish primrose flower on the heaths and machair, heather colours the hills and clumps of pink thrift carpet parts of the coast.

These are fertile isles. A wealth of fishing awaits the angler, and if you are one of those for whom angling is part of the larger experience of man and nature, a visit to the Orkney Isles will leave you happily enriched.

Chapter 10

Dumfriesshire

Surprising South-West

Dumfriesshire, including Nithsdale, is part of what is often known as 'Scotland's Surprising South-West', and is just that. Surprising. Interesting facts abound.

Dumfries. Well, Robert the Bruce murdered John Comyn here. Arbigland, to the south, was the birthplace of John Paul Jones, the founder of the American Navy. Sanquhar, north, has Britain's oldest post office. Ecclefechan was the home of Thomas Carlyle; Gretna famous for runaway marriages, Moffat, holder of several 'Britain in Bloom' awards, was a Victorian spa town; and Wanlockhead, with its Museum of Lead Mining, is Scotland's highest village. As if that wasn't enough to halt the visitor heading north on the A74 with no thought in his head but to make for the Highlands, let us not forget that Dumfriesshire, for part of his life, was Robert Burns country. In June 1787 he was made an honorary burgess of 'honest Dumfries' and the following Whitsunday he moved into the farm at Ellisland, close to the River Nith. Times were not always easy for him there and he loved to ease the pressure with a wander along the riverbank. As ever, he felt compelled to write a few lines describing his feelings.

November Nith
salmon

'As on the banks of winding Nith,
Ae smiling simmer-morn I stray'd,
And traced its bonnie howes and haughs,
Where linties sang and lambkins play'd,
I sat me down upon a craig,
And drank my fill o' fancy's dream
When, from the eddying deep below,
Uprose the genius of the stream.'

This was the first verse of a poem subtitled 'On the Destruction of the Woods near Drumlanrig'. But I'm sure Robert would be glad to know that nowadays destruction is far from the present Duke of Buccleuch's thoughts. Indeed, quite the opposite. Rural harmony has actively been sought on the estate for the last 150 years. A wide variety of tree species has been planted and a mixture of age-groups is also important in providing suitable habitat for a range of plants, animals, birds and insects. Wet places, bogs and small lochs are all part of this harmony, and there are some 20 man-made lochs in the area. The theory seems to be effective too, as the biggest sycamore in Britain is alive and well in the park near Drumlanrig Castle. It is 300 years old and quietly absorbs 600 tons of water a year. And the first Douglas Fir, planted in 1832 after having been sent home from North America by Douglas himself to his brother, who was Master of Works at Drumlanrig, is still alive and well. Threads of the past, impinging on the present day.

On a sunny and breezy late-autumn morning, the Nith was, as ever, winding its way through the Queensberry Estate, and, after overnight rain, it was nicely coloured. The trees of Drumlanrig were in their autumn livery, the wind shedding some of the leaves into the river. It was late in the season, 5 November, and I was expecting fireworks. The Nith, like some other Borders rivers, fishes almost into the winter of the year, and in this late spate there was a good chance of a fish. The Nith has produced some heavy fish over the years, but none to beat that which was reputedly landed by Jock Wallace, a well-known local poacher. He was on the Clog Pool of Barjarg Water one morning in 1812 when he hooked a big fish. It led him a fairly dour dance for a long time and eventually took him downriver to the Barjarg Boat Pool, where it was gaffed by some workmen. The fish had been hooked at 8 a.m. and was at last on the bank at 6 p.m., with only two strands of Wallace's horsehair cast remaining intact. The fish was immediately taken to Barjarg Tower and weighed in the presence of Mr Hunter Arundell, the proprietor. He and other witnesses signed a certificate of the weight, a copy of which is still in the family. We don't know if Jock was actually fishing with the permission of Mr Arundell, but we do know that the fish weighed 67 pounds. And on a horsehair cast and probably a home-made rod.

I was not expecting to catch any such monster, and after a fruitless hour with the fly rod, catching an interesting selection of leaves, my companion, John MacMillan, suggested that a cast or two on the lower pool with a spinner might move a fish. Since John had been a ghillie on the estate for many years and knew the water well, I did as he suggested and quite quickly hooked a fish. After a bit of a sprauchle, it was safely netted by John. A slightly coloured 6½-pounder on the Toby. Perhaps no great catch by today's standards, but I was delighted – and if you go back to the turn of the century, it would have been considered a minor miracle to catch such a fish.

The River Nith suffered badly around that time. What with fish being taken by the whammle, paidle and haaf nets, obstacles such as the Cauld at Dumfries making it difficult for fish to run the river, and pollution, it is hardly surprising that few fish were caught by the rods. The river took sewage and mill and factory effluent, and in 1891 a netsman gave this statement to the Clerk of the Nith District Board: 'When the river is low, I consider the pollutions the sole cause of deterioration. Scarcely a fish will run up, and I have seen them at the ford at the New Quay making back to the sea after meeting the refuse from the mills. The dyes are plainly seen in the water: they are of various colours at different times – black, violet, drab – and at Castle Dykes I have seen several colours at one time. During six weeks of drought, I have seen the water black from bank to bank; so black that a piece of white paper could not be seen a foot deep and what with the sewage and mill effluents, the smell is so bad that I could compare the river to nothing but a stinking canal.'

And ten years later, a gentleman wrote to a friend, 'I am afraid that salmon fishing on the Nith is entirely done for. It is full of pike and grayling which ought to be destroyed, but the proprietors appear to take no interest in the river, as few of them are anglers. For the last seven years it has been going back yearly and 1900 was the very worst on record with not a dozen fish taken from the whole river.'

So the 'good old days' weren't quite so good on the Nith, and everyone will be glad to see that since those bad old days a hundred years ago the river has been cleaned up and the salmon are running again. Let's hope this modern generation is prepared to continue with the good work so that the fish will still be running a hundred years from now. Like that sycamore and Douglas's Douglas Fir, we owe it to our children.

This part of Scotland is one of the most productive for the country's ever-growing band of coarse fishermen. I remember many years ago hearing of the Castle Loch at Lochmaben and its shoals of bream, and of Loch Ken and the pike. If I remember rightly, the Hydro people trapped over 20 tons of pike there in the early 1970s. But there are numerous other waters with coarse fish in them. I have a note in an old diary of visiting friends at Rockcliffe and digging some nice brandling worms from a fairly pongy dung-heap and tottering happily off to the White Loch at the top of the road. Fishing with the old-fashioned, springy, vivid-green Luron 2 nylon (I never knew what happened to Luron 1), a wee cork float painted red and a couple of the worms as bait, I took over a dozen perch up to half a pound. I probably gave them to our friends as a gesture of appreciation, so they moved house shortly afterwards.

Lochrutton Loch is a popular fishery and all over the area there are

waters with roach, bream, perch and pike. We met two chaps up from the north of England for one of their regular pike forays. We got chatting about what it was that brought them time and again back to Scotland when they had pike in their local waters. It was the fighting quality of the fish that seemed to tip the balance for them. That, coupled with the surroundings. I asked if they had ever caught the same fish twice and was assured that some fish had been caught up to nine times. I wondered how they recognised the fish each time, and learned that all pike have different markings, rather like human fingerprints. These fellows always return their fish carefully, with the minimum of stress, as they would never think of killing a pike. It seems to do the fish no lasting harm, as the nine-times-caught 'Nelson' proves. This fish has only got one eye, and as the guys said, 'When he comes out of the water, he even has a smile on his chops, ready for the camera. He's been caught that often, he's the only pike we've ever seen with a flipping suntan!'

The area also is bountifully speckled with lochs for the wild brown trout fisher, but we decided to go to one of the more interesting man-made fisheries. The Moffat Fishery is one of the few places where anglers in this country have a chance to lock lures with *Salvelinus fontinalis*, the American brook trout, a handsome fish with a mottled yellow back and distinctive white piping on the front edges of the pectoral, pelvic and anal fins (all those underneath ones!). Being more closely related to char than trout, the brookies need a constant supply of cool, clean water, which is where Moffat scores. Natural springs produce what feels like cool water in summer and relatively warm water in winter. Brown and rainbow trout are also reared and stocked at Moffat, so whenever you fish there, you are secure in the knowlege that the three species can be tempted to take your fly.

Fishery manager Peter Hesketh took me through part of the day's work. First thing, there was the stocking of new fish to make good the previous day's catches. We netted one of the holding ponds, loaded the fish into a bin and took them to the main fishing pond on the back of the pick-up. They were gently eased into the water and, having made sure that they all swam off safely, the next job was to go round all the tanks and ponds to feed the three species in their various stages of growth. The pellets that cause the feeding frenzy, a mini matanza, are high in protein, with fibre, colour and all the other bits and pieces that hatchery-bred fish require to keep them healthy.

Then, after a general check-up of the fishery to make sure all was well, I was allowed to fish for an hour or two. A floating line, with a long 5-pound leader and barbless damsel nymph inched back, after giving the lure time to sink, was initially effective in inducing a fish to smash the cast on the take. All I saw was the fly-line jag momentarily, and, when I tightened, there was a moment of solid resistance, and the cast was broken. Whether it was a big fish, a lack of technique or a poorly tied knot, I know not. But the fish was gone. I retied and retried. A few casts later, the leader shot away again and I was into a fish. In the net, my first Moffat brookie was a real butterball of a fish. Barbless hooks make for an easy return to the water and the fish swam off strongly. Next, a rainbow, full finned and thickly tailed, took the same barbless nymph, came to the net, and was returned. A change of tactics – a Daddy-Long-Legs fished dry – induced a beautiful head and tail rise which I thought at first might be another brookie, but which turned out to be a brown trout of about 2½ pounds. That, too, after a few moments taken to admire the rich, deep brown colouring and chunky shape, was returned safely and swam off strongly. Three fish, three separate species. A delightful couple of hours – and vindication, should it be needed, of the pleasure to be had for the angler from well-organised man-made fisheries.

Back at Drumlanrig, there are many opportunities for the family to have a day out together, and I'm sure few would not enjoy the spectacle of birds of prey being flown; the ancient art of falconry. The Drumlanrig Birds of Prey Centre allows you to get close to some magnificent hawks and falcons, both indigenous Scottish birds and their relatives from around the world. Russian Steppe eagles, goshawks, peregrine falcons and South American harris hawks are all put through their paces for visitors. Their keeper, Alistair McKissock, took me out with Hazel and Lucy, two Harris hawks, as he put them through their rabbit-catching routine on a Dumfriesshire hillside. A day on the hill is exhilarating enough, but with a hawk on the wrist, waiting for a rabbit to bolt, that excitement is heightened. Man and bird are stationed uphill of the prey, and as the rabbit scurries for its burrow, the hawk slides from the wrist and glides down towards the quarry. If the rabbit is smart, it runs uphill as the hawks cannot turn and match its speed, so roughly only one in four flights is successful, the rabbit usually managing to turn away from its pursuer. To see these large birds on the wing in the open Scottish countryside is a thrilling sight.

To see dark brown mud squelching up between your toes is perhaps less thrilling but nonetheless interesting in a tactile sense. To take part in the World Flounder Tramping Championships it was necessary to bare all from thigh down and sensitise toes to the touch of flatfish underfoot. Organiser Harry Ellis told me that the whole idea sprang from a little local rivalry between a couple of Palnackie lads as to who could tramp the bigger flounder and, since no one else had thought of it before and more and more people wanted to join the fun, they decided to give it the 'World' title. Palnackie sits on a creek of the Rough Firth near the estuary of the Urr Water. At low tide vast mudflats are laid bare and the idea is to plowter across these acres of mud until you reach the channel of the Urr, and then, quite simply, tramp flatties.

Well, as with so many things, it is not actually as simple as it sounds. Picture it for yourself. You are wading knee-deep in murky water – you can't see the bottom – and suddenly you feel something alive squirming under your foot. What is the first thing you'll probably do? That's right. Lift your foot. And where will the squirmy thing be now? That's right. Gone. And if that happens, what chance have you got of being World Champion? That's right. None. So a great deal of anti-lifting-your-foot-when-you-feel-a-squirmy-thing resolve has to be summoned up and has also to be applied to the feel of crab underfoot or on end of toe. The water was surprisingly warm and several flounders had been taken. Some folk tried to enhance their chances by wearing wetsuits to keep them warm or socks to keep the sensation of crab-nips to a minimum. Softies all. The true tramper does it naked – feet anyway. It is definitely an odd feeling, though. Putting each foot firmly down and resolving not to move it if something is felt. But you get used to it after a while and the whole experience was highly enjoyable, even if I did finish flounderless. At the weigh-in, wouldn't you know, it was a woman who had won. Moira Slater from Dalbeattie had a flounder of 2 pounds 1 ounce to claim the world title. I blamed my lack of success on the fact that even if I do have flat feet, I obviously don't have flattie feet.

Chapter 11

STIRLINGSHIRE

Going Forth into the Teith

As it meanders past Barbadoes, Offrins of Gartut and Pendicles of Collymoon, Faraway, Cambusdrenny and North Kersebonny, a gently rolling stream that gathers three Mosses, Gartrenich, Flanders and Drip, you might be forgiven for thinking that this is just a wee Scottish river, bothering no one on its way to the sea. Wrong. This is the river which, joined by the Teith just above Stirling, is known the world over. Augustus Grimble deems it to be the fifth-largest of the Scottish rivers, and I know it is the Forth.

It is born from two streams, the Duchray Water rolling out of Loch Ard Forest, and a small, dark burn, Avondhu, issuing from Loch Ard itself. From Aberfoyle to Stirling, it is hardly the archetypal Scottish river. A trifle sluggish in places, deep and dark. It is not really a trouty-looking water, more suited, you'd imagine, to coarse fish. True, roach and perch and pike can be taken, but there are trout to be caught and, in season, some salmon will turn at a spinner or be willing to take a well-presented worm.

The Teith is the product of two main systems, coming from some of the most beautiful parts of Scotland. Eas Gobhain is the end product of waters running from the hills into Loch Katrine, Loch Achray and Loch Venachar, and just above Callander it meets water from the Braes of Balquhidder which comes through Loch Doine and Loch Voil, then the bonny Strathyre Forest and Loch Lubnaig to tumble through the Pass and Falls of Leny.

This is a river of much more interest to the game fisher than the Forth. Running clear normally, with a greenish tinge after rain, catches have improved in recent years and there are day-tickets available for some excellent water in Callander. Town water is often looked down on, but on opening day here it is not unlikely for several springers to be landed – good fish too, in the 12- to 15-pound class. A great fan of the Teith is Peter Anderson, who knows the river well and has taken a considerable number of fish off it over the years. He likes the ambience of the river, the fact that it is available for the price of a permit and a chance of getting a fish any day throughout the lengthy season, stretching from 1 February to the end of October. We fished the town water early in the season and Peter cast a lightly weighted wooden minnow across the likely lies and we watched it flutter back to his feet. It looked tempting indeed, but the fish thought otherwise.

Peter is a world casting champion, and that means he is the best in the world. I know that sounds simple, but think about it. No one in the world is as good as him.

He took me to a particularly attractive bit of fly water, too shallow

Peter Anderson demonstrates at the Game Fair

for the spinner and with a lovely draw for the fly. I covered a fish he'd seen splashing in a lie in the fast water. I fished conventionally – down and across – through the pool, then Peter came in behind me. It was a revelation to watch a man so completely in control. He showed how to fish square, to control the speed of the fly, pulling it tantalisingly away from a fish, inducing it to follow, rather than letting the fly hang over it. It's not just his casting ability that impresses, but the way he can lead a fly across the current, dropping the rod tip to slow the fly or raising the rod for a faster presentation. He does all this in complete sympathy with the river to make the fly fish as he wishes, and watching him try many variations made me realise how jaded, how unimaginative my own fishing had become.

The same with the spinner. A thoughtful choice of lure – perhaps a wooden Devon minnow fished on a dropper above the weight, so that it can be fished slowly, or a small Toby, but half-painted a colour Peter knows will make the lure more effective – often produces fish in difficult conditions. He'll take up a wee spinning rod he's had for 20 years and flick that small Toby out and across the stream and do the same thing as with the fly, leading the bait as he wants, not as the speed of the river dictates. We fished together again a few weeks later in mid-March, a day of squalls, bright sunshine then swirling snow showers reminding us that it was, indeed, still early in the year. The river was in good nick after rain, but fish were scarce. He had a favourite spot, a lie almost opposite the Roman Camp Hotel. Out went that painted Toby and Peter produced the goods. A 7-pound springer, sea-lice newly off it, was nipped out of that lie. It can be a mite frustrating watching other people catch fish when you feel you have persevered enough to be due one yourself, but that is never the case when watching Peter. You appreciate the skill of the man and, if you are wise, you strive to emulate, not envy his artistry.

But we don't always have a Peter Anderson on hand to magic fish out for the camera. Left to me, it can often take a wee bit longer and that's when we start to get silly. Where the two rivers join, the Teith seems the larger river, the real river, so the Forth might be the false Teith. Neville thought bait fishers might get a good bite from the Teith and Ricky decided we should find an angling dentist, so that we could both fish the mouth of the Teith. There are some fine bridges on the Teith, the river is unpolluted – nice to see clean Teith – and if you don't catch a fish, well, there's no need to feel down in the mouth, just brush up your Teith techniques, drill out that bait and you might catch an amalgam of salmon and sea trout for which you'll deserve a plaque.

But there is no joking about the fishing. We arrived one late-October morning just below that confluence where Forth and Teith become one. There is a very popular spot near where the motorway crosses the river and anglers were out in numbers. But Bill Wiseman had moved upstream away from the crowd and was fishing what looked like featureless water below the road bridge, when a large salmon came out of the reeds, thwacked the Toby and gave him problems. He normally carries a tailer, but sport had been slow on the previous two or three days so he hadn't bothered to bring it. Being in a fairly public spot though, help, if not at hand immediately, was soon delivered in the shape of a net from downstream, delivered by an out-of-breath angler, and Bill, with advice coming from every quarter, eventually drew a big cock fish over the rim. On the scales, it registered 21 pounds – a fish to make anyone's season. In autumn colours, tartan some say, it was proof that big fish do still run the river. Old records note netsmen taking fish over 50 pounds. 58 being the heaviest – and one wonders if these were Forth or Teith fish.

While Bill was taking his fish, the patience of Rita Thomson had been rewarded. She was fishing a huge bunch of worms, at least half a dozen on the hook. A water bailiff on the River Nairn had taught her how to do it and it had proved successful on many occasions. One Friday evening, she had taken three fish one after the other from the same spot – day-ticket water, remember. They weighed 11, 16 and 19½ pounds – and this from a woman who doesn't even start fishing until the bowling season is over! But she had just caught one fish today, 27 October, and what a beauty it was: 6 or 7 pounds and covered in long-tailed sea-lice, it showed tangibly that fresh fish are running right to the end of that long season.

And the catching of salmon can, quite legally, continue into November, this time not to take something out of the river but to put something back. High in the hills above Doune, somewhere between Loch Mahaick and Corscaplie, we made our way to the head of a small tributary of the Allan Water, itself a tributary of the Forth. We were being taken electro fishing by a fine body of men, under the supervision of Salmon Fisheries Board Superintendent, Ian Baird. The idea is to capture mature hen and cock fish, transport them back to the hatchery and, when mature, to strip them of eggs and milt. The fertilised eggs are cared for over winter until hatching and the fry eventually introduced to the burns at the optimum time.

Electro fishing is a relatively harmless way to take fish. The idea is to wade the river and probe likely salmon lies with a diode, a long pole with a metal ring, and if it comes near a fish, it receives a charge of DC current – with stunning results – allowing it to be netted and retained with a minimum of damage and stress. The several hen fish we took, 5 or 6 pounds in weight, had made a long journey into the hills and, left undisturbed in the river to let nature take its course, might have produced five to six thousand eggs. In the wild, though, mortality is high in the early stages of life, and once hatched, fewer than one in a thousand might reach maturity. The hatchery gives a measure of control and protection to the vulnerable ova, allowing a better percentage of eggs to survive that first, dangerous winter. After the fish are stripped, they are slipped back into the river, where, with a bit of luck, they will make it back to sea, blissfully unaware that their progeny have a better chance of returning as mature fish to populate the same rivers and burns. It was a fascinating day of bright sunshine and we saw sea trout, some of which looked as though they had already spawned, and a goodly number of parr, proof that conditions in the burn were promising for the artificially hatched fish on their reintroduction. The salmon we took were dark in colour, normal for a peaty burn at that time of year, with roughly the right proportion of cocks to hens, and Ian declared himself happy with the day's enterprise. It was good to see so many committed anglers putting so much time into efforts to help in the preservation of a species we all admire and respect.

On our way off the hills, Stirling Castle and the Wallace Monument were standing proud in the violet sky of the gloaming. History everywhere. The castle was recaptured from the English in 1297 after the Battle of Stirling Bridge by William Wallace. James II was born here in 1430 and James V in 1512. Mary, Queen of Scots and James VI spent time here. The Hereditary Keeper of the Castle is the Earl of Mar and Kellie and the view from the 420-foot-high Queen Victoria's Look-Out extends well into the Highlands – Stirling has long been known as 'The Gateway to the Highlands'. Visit the castle and be reminded plangently of Scotland's history. Climb Abbey Craig, 362 feet high and topped by the 220-foot-high Wallace Monument. Erected in 1869 at a cost of £16,000, it contains Wallace's sword. Go to the Kilsyth Hills, the Campsie Fells and the Fintry Hills, climb Conic, Ben Vrackie and Ben Lomond and you are still in Stirlingshire. Stop off for a wander in Kippen or Killearn, Balfron or Buchlyvie, or Balmaha and Rowardennan

Dave Crossley with that wild carp from Culcreuch Castle Loch

on Loch Lomondside.

As I've mentioned earlier, Loch Lomond has a varied head of coarse fish, but as far as I know wild carp don't turn up very often. In a pond beside Culcreuch Castle near Fintry, however, they do. This lovely little water is run by the Scottish Carp Group, who take great care of this precious asset. Mind you, when we arrived, it was raining fit to burst and several members of the Group were sheltering under their brollies, waiting for the floats to make a move. But Dave Crossley's day had started well. In the early-morning sunshine, the fish were feeding well and several species had been taken – roach, perch, rudd and, most excitingly, a wild carp. Dave had hooked the carp well out from his peg and the fish had weeded him. Never one to panic, Dave took a risk and slackened off, hoping the fish would swim free by itself. He waited patiently and that is just what happened. The fish was landed and kept for us to look at. A beautiful burnished gold, with the characteristic barbels at the mouth, it was a handsome fish, powerfully built, and a welcome addition to the stock of this water. Dave was happy to return it, safe in the knowledge that it wasn't living there alone.

The many meanders of the Forth around Gargunnock and Drip Moss also find favour with the coarse angler. Here you can spin or bait fish for pike – double-figure fish can be expected now and again, and perch and shoals of roach, when located, can give fast and furious sport.

The trout angler has variety to choose from with Carron Valley and North Third reservoirs giving contrasting sport. Boat fish for free-rising (sometimes!) brown trout at Carron or bank fish for thumping rainbows at North Third. That's the great thing about Scotland. These two waters are about five miles apart as the crow flies – Peter Anderson could probably cast from one to the other – and they are quite different.

Another place which deserves a mention when we are talking trout is Howietoun, the result of the scientific foresight of one man, Sir James Maitland. He believed that fish could be farmed in the same way as cattle and sheep, but at the time, the 1870s, those who had tried fish-farming had done so in an unscientific and random way. Sir James, experimenting over a number of years, developed Howietoun into an innovative and efficient scientific enterprise. He started by using portable ponds, but found that flood water could float them away. He then built a hatching-house taking great care that the water going to the hatching-boxes was filtered free of all sediment. He believed suspended particles were responsible for many mortalities, a belief proved by experiments at

Howietoun a hundred years later. It was discovered that if ponds were not built at right angles to the prevailing winds, the fry were more susceptible to fungus. As the enterprise grew, feeding the trout was a major exercise. Sheep carcasses and rabbit liver were tried, but the fry thrived on pellets cut from a thick paste of hard-boiled eggs and meat. Older fish were fed a minced mixture of shellfish, mussels and clams, and horsemeat.

Sir James was experimenting, expanding and exporting. He pioneered methods of successfully sending Loch Leven ova to New Zealand in iced trays hung in a swansdown bag insulated with sawdust. Sphagnum moss round the boxes of trays was crucial in maintaining the required temperature on the long journey. His workers wore silk overalls, being smoother and softer than tweed, and he employed women using quill feathers to dress the eggs in the hatching-house. His work was recognised with the award of medals and diplomas, and when he died in 1897 the impact of his work was seen worldwide, hatcheries in Kenya, India, New Zealand and South Africa showing influences of Howietoun.

From then until the 1960s, the fishery was commercially successful, there being heavy demand for brown trout to stock the many new fisheries that had sprung up to meet the increased demand for angling. Then there was a period when the whole facility was in danger of closure due to a series of misfortunes, but in 1979 it was bought by Stirling University. Under its present director, Dr Derek Robertson, Howietoun is once again supplying high-quality brown trout for restocking, and students of the university's Institute of Aquaculture come to the fishery as part of the teaching programme. It is good to know that Sir James Maitland's foresight and zeal are being fostered by those who care and share his vision to maintain Howietoun as the cradle of the world's scientific study of fish-farming, and as such, well deserved of a wider recognition in Scotland's angling history.

We finished up our Stirlingshire-Central Region programme with another visit to that lovely fishery, the Lake of Menteith, in the company of a most splendid bunch of jokers, the Lame Ducks Angling Club, so-called because the members are all disabled in some way. It is not always easy for club members to get out onto the water, but at the Lake, access to boats is good and Bill Martindale and his staff will do all they can to get the chaps safely aboard. Boat fishing means they have to have an able-bodied person aboard, and as I just qualified, I was to ghillie for Rab Mitchell and Frank Reilly. Andrew Herd and Bert Sneddon were in the

*The Lame Ducks –
and spot the booby!*

other boat and there was quite a bit of banter going on. Andrew is a well-known fly-tier and a great man for the birds – I mean he can whistle you down a siskin or a bullfinch, having years of experience of breeding song-birds.

There are over thirty members of the club with different disabilities, some limbless and some deaf and dumb. Disabled they may be, but they can fish and help each other. Someone who has lost a lower limb can still tie a fly onto a cast for someone without an arm, and it is this spirit that shines through. Fish were caught by all the members that day, a couple by most, four by Bert. As we totted up the final catch, it did not go unnoticed that I had caught nothing, nix, zero, zilch. This lowly position deserved nothing other than the booby prize – a giant Booby-nymph tied by Andrew Herd. I looked in a magazine to see the description of a Booby. Designed to be fished 'close to the bottom', it said. Since that was where I figured in the list of catches, I accepted the prize. But it hurt!

Chapter 12

ARGYLL AND LOCH AWE

Records and Rainbows

Argyll, on Scotland's west coast, is an area of breathtaking scenery. Loch Fyne and Loch Etive push their way saltily to the heart of this beautiful county and Loch Awe is the fresh-water finger threading through some of the most staggering country in Scotland, dominated by mighty peaks such as the Cobbler and the Munros of Ben Ime and Ben Cruachan.

There are rivers with salmon, others once more famous for their sea trout, lochs with brown trout and coarse fish and an infinitely varied coastline offering shore and boat anglers a real salt-water challenge. Here, there is a chance for the angler with transport, motorised or of the Shanks's Pony variety, to spend time in the best of all possible ways: trying for a big trout or pike in Loch Awe, a salmon from the River Awe, rainbow trout in the more comfortable surroundings of Inverawe Fisheries or just gently fishing from Inveraray pier and the shores of Loch Fyne on a summer evening for hard-fighting mackerel on light spinning tackle. You need never be short of an opportunity for a cast or two in Argyll.

I had fished the River Fyne for a number of years. A delightful little water, always the better of a wee bit of rain to give decent flow. The Victorians had done some remarkable work, creating deep pools from shallow riffles by cunning use of croys and weirs and in good condition,

Two Fyne salmon: James Hay and I at Black Bridge

you could not wish to fish a more pleasant river.

Some lovely fly water and, with the permission of the keeper, in the right water conditions you are also allowed to fish the worm in some of the deep pools and chasms where the fly is inaccessible. The day we fished the Fyne, it was wet, very wet – just ideal. The river was in spate, nicely coloured, and after having no luck on one of my favourite pools on the lower beat, Ballingall's, just above the sea pool, we went upstream to fish the Black Bridge. With the cameras all set up, I decided to go in at the top of the deep, narrow run under the bridge which then opens out into one of those pools where the weir at the tail creates good resting water for fish which have run through thinnish, rocky water, over the top of the weir and into the pool. Peter Manson, a man who patently loves his river, had always told me to fish the fly right to the lip, as fish would often lie there after their hard journey. So I decided to wet the fly at the neck and get into my rhythm before fishing down to the best of the water. As so often happens, a fish took at the least expected moment. The fly was wet, fishing nicely and I was reeling in to make my way under the

bridge, when the line shot away and a fish was on. At the same moment, I realised that the river was that bit higher than normal, and knew that I couldn't wade through under the bridge. I was stuck. And if that wasn't bad enough, my landing net was safely stowed in the boot of my car. Great!

The Falls of Lora

It is interesting that since the Argyll programme was shown, with me making a bit of a doolie of myself trying to land the fish, only a couple of people, both ladies I may say, have asked why I didn't get one of the film crew to go back to the car for the landing net. Good question. But *I* had forgotten to bring it and it seemed to me that *I* should be left to shoulder the burden of that lapse. If I lost the fish it would be my own fault, and I would have learned a severe lesson always to make sure I took my net; and if I managed to land it, well, there might just be a bit of fun to be caught on camera. As it happened, I made a bit of a hash of landing it by hand, hampered somewhat, I may say in my own defence, by the Black Bridge itself. Three or four times I think it took me, but I was more satisfied to overcome the difficulties of being netless than I would have

113

been if one of the crew had thrown me the lifeline of my landing net. And I think it was more exciting to watch. It wasn't big, a cock fish of about 6 pounds, but I did land it and it will for ever seem to me to be a fine Fyne salmon indeed!

As I have said, this part of Argyll is dominated by three lochs, two salt- and one fresh-water. The sea angler has a great variety of water to explore.

Loch Fyne, from its upper reaches at the mouth of the River Fyne (try the excellent Oyster Bar and sea-food restaurant there) to where it joins the Firth of Clyde via the Sound of Bute and the Kilbrannan Sound on the west side of the Isle of Arran, offers the shore and boat angler a variety of fishing opportunities. Though famous in the past for its vast shoals of herring, it is now less productive on a larger scale but still an area where the innovative angler can enjoy the challenge of inshore fishing.

Loch Etive gives a different challenge. It is a bit of an oddity: a deep, almost landlocked salt-water loch. With each tide, the Falls of Lora only allow a modest influx of fresh salt water, if you know what I mean, and exit of stale salt water, so the introduction of new water is minimal. Also, Hughie Smith found to his cost that fresh water from the many burns and rivers coming into the loch tends to sit on top of the salt when his precious ragworm reacted violently to a change of water taken from near the surface. It is even said that brown trout inhabit the upper layer of fresh water in an intrinsically salt-water environment, so it may come as little surprise that in this somewhat unusual loch, the species of fish found tend to live a different life from their ocean brethren. Given the fact that we caught mackerel in February, gurnard which seem comfortable there all year round, packs of dogfish finding Etive a home in which there is enough feeding and from which they feel little need to roam, and an occasional thornback ray, Loch Etive seems to be a unique saline microcosm – even hake have been taken here.

Fish that shouldn't be where they are at that time of year are happy to be there all year round because conditions are propitious. An oddball of a place and all the more interesting for that. An outing with someone like Ronnie Campbell at any time of year can prove an interesting day, testing both belief and technique. Try it!

For the game fisher, the major challenge is Loch Awe. We fished it many times and on the less productive days re-christened it many different names, one of the few printable ones being Loch NaeuseatAwe! But that was our fault for being there at the wrong time. There are many anglers who have had halcyon days on this beautiful water, for trout, pike and salmon.

The story of the new British record brown trout, taken from the loch by that splendid band of loonies, the Ferox 85 Group, follows later. And Freddie Sutherland and I had our eyes opened on the opening day for the trout fishing when our search for early-season brown trout was happily interrupted by the capture of a couple of good rainbow trout. Yes, they were escapees from the cages on the loch, but it seems these rainbows have now become part of the Loch Awe angling experience, and to catch a couple of decent fish on a day of snow showers and attendant meteorological rainbows, was thrill enough.

The regular pike fishers have their favourite haunts on Loch Awe side, too. We happened along on a couple of times which coincided with anglers' few blank days – leading us to suggest another alternative name for the water, Loch NaefishatAwe – but sometimes we were there when anglers were on form and fish were on the feed and some beautiful pike were taken.

I happen to get the same thrill from seeing a well-conditioned pike of around 20 pounds as I do from a salmon of the same weight, and Loch Awe can give the dedicated pike angler some memorable days. Mike Maule, Eric Paterson, Mike Fairley and Colin Campbell all took fish of decent proportions, up to 19 pounds. They are dedicated, careful and caring anglers who leave no rubbish or discarded tackle and are always in possession of permission or permit as necessary for where they fish. Mike Maule even brings a bag to cart away detritus left by less responsible so-called anglers. It was delightful to be in their company and to see them catch fish for the camera, if only to show that the knowledgeable angler can change the name of this loch to Loch NaebotheratAwe!

The River Awe is another kettle of fish, literally. In the past, it was the mightiest salmon river in Scotland – the nearest we had to the rivers of Norway. At Taychreggan, there is a cast of a 56-pound fish taken in 1923 by Mr H.G. Thornton. He was one of only three men who landed two salmon over 50 pounds in their lifetime, two of whom took their fish from the Awe and the other from the Wye.

After our programme on this part of Argyll was shown, Mr Thornton's daughter, Diana, wrote to me with a beautifully detailed account of her father's capture of the 56-pounder, the 51-pounder and other memorable fish. With her permission, I'll give you an impression

115

of those epic days.

Mr Thornton took the fishing on the Awe in 1923. He described it as 'a very strongly flowing river, more than a very long cast across in many places: very rocky and when in spate it tears along with a lot of white water showing. Its banks are rough going and when a good fish tries to go out of a pool, there is no stopping him. He uses all his might in the strong water and fights downward all the time. In 1923, I began fishing on June 1st in good water conditions and on the 4th had five salmon, 16 to 19 pounds, a notable catch. On the 6th, a 42-pound fish took a 3/0 'Bulldog', a perfectly shaped fish which was safely gaffed by ghillie Sam MacIntyre. I sent it off to Malloch's of Perth to be set up.'

Mr Thornton describes Awe fish as being well proportioned: short, thick and small-headed. The 42-pound salmon would be the fish of a lifetime for the modern angler, but worthy of only a passing mention in these days of big fish. Better, says Mr Thornton, was still to come.

Mr Thornton, with a good crowd watching, plays the 56-pounder

'On June 12th, after a rise in water, I was fishing Pol Verie with a large Green Highlander in drizzling rain, and near the tail of the pool I

had a heavy dead pull. Nothing moved for a second or two, but when I lifted my rod, an 18-foot spliced Grant, and put some strain on, the fish moved out into the waves and after a turn upstream, he went off downstream, boring right out of the pool into the Little Verie, then down the rapids. This meant a run at top speed for me with my rod held high as possible to clear the rocks. I had all my fly-line out with the silk backing cutting into my fingers.'

They were hardy in those days. Mr Thornton was wielding an 18-foot Grant rod, probably the famous Grant Vibration, no lightweight, at the age of 54 and I know of few present-day anglers who would find that an easy challenge. Couple it with a heavy river, difficult to wade and negotiate, and a big fish, and his achievement becomes greater. The fight went on, the fish dropping downriver all the while.

'Presently he took up a position behind a big rock which had the main current running on the far side of it. It would have been "Goodbye" if he went that way, so I held him very hard and worried him for an hour.'

An hour? A whole hour? And that's just part of the fight. I have never even had the privilege of playing a salmon large enough to test me for anything approaching an hour!

'Things were looking better and drawing him to my side, I let him down a series of falls not far from me, but I had a cliff above me and some bad scrambling under trees, but I was pretty confident now that I should get him in the Bothy Pool. This had been difficult going for some time, but now I came to a grass track with no need to hurry, so I started to swing him to my side, still upright in the water, and in a small quiet bay, drew him inwards. Sam, leaning over a rock, had a good chance to gaff him square, as the fish's head rested between two rocks and I caught Sam, nearly 70 years old, by the coat so that he shouldn't fall in, and out he lifted the best fish of my life. A great fight, lasting two and a half hours and ending five hundred yards from where he was hooked. I took him into Taynuilt to be weighed roughly and sent him off to Malloch of Perth to be set up. He made 56 pounds the next day, was 52 inches long and 29 in girth. He had spent two years in the river and four years feeding in the sea. Two ladies, who had been looking on from the opposite bank and had brought me luck, drove me to Taynuilt and I took back a bottle of Giesler to celebrate!'

And so would I, whatever Giesler is. Mr Thornton had the grace to admit that the following day he lent the beat to a friend because he was 'stiff in the shoulders'.

117

Eleven years later, he was back on his beloved Awe. On 25 April he had a 'proper beauty of 32 pounds on a Silver Devon', and a day or two later, fishing a prawn on his 18-foot Castle Connel, he had a hard pull in the Seal pool, and was into a heavy fish. He worked it in the pool for some 20 minutes when it bolted out into the centre of the river, making for the Pol Nugan rocks. The fish went down the falls with Mr Thornton going all out, full speed down the bank beside the long Verie falls, up a steep path on to the road above and bringing the fish, plunging and splashing, into quieter water near his bank. John Jack, the ghillie, got the gaff into the fish and it was landed.

'I knew I had a whopper, but he was heavier than I thought as he bumped down my 50-pound scales and when I took him to the village and station, I found he weighed 51 pounds. This was beyond what I ever expected to do with big fish since it was eleven years since I had the 56-pounder. These two, taken from a fast-flowing river, full of rocks, in grand scenery gave me the highest one can expect in salmon fishing. Some people ask if I have had other big fish on or risen. Well, it is difficult to say. It was in my 68th year that I hooked a fish just below the Brander Burn on 5/5 gut which splashed on the surface. I said to my ghillie, Jim Jack, "That's a monster." Suffice to say that five and a quarter hours later' [yes, five and a quarter hours!] 'when I lost the fish, opinion was that it was nearer 60 pounds than 50. But I have always said that on a river like the Awe, two hooked out of three on the bank, is good work, so I leave it at that.'

My only wish is that we had had the chance to fish that river in its great days. Imagine what a wonderful filming sequence we could have had with Mr Thornton fishing his 18-foot rods for these magnificent salmon. But I am grateful to him for his vibrant descriptions of great Awe days past.

Nonetheless, Argyll and the Awes, Loch and River, should nowadays be in every angler's mind as an area to explore and enjoy – and who knows, like Mr Thornton and, as you will shortly find out, the Ferox 85 Group, you may also find yourself in the record books.

As Ron Greer is about to explain, the new British record brown trout did not just happen along. Many hundreds of hours were spent by these dedicated anglers in pursuit of a quarry they knew could be found in this great system.

The man himself, Mr H.B. Thornton

Relentless Road to a Record

Trolling for the Salmo Ferox: It's a far cry to Loch Awe. These are the title and sub-title on page 377 of a book called *The Moor and the Loch* written by Sir John Colqhoun of Luss and published in 1880. This book, as well as giving an insight into the sporting and cultural attitudes of the Victorian upper classes, is something of a ferox-fisher's bible. It is part of a period publication on, and practice in, the art of wangling out wild whopper trout from Highland lochs. It was a period that made these leviathans into legends and which fired at least one wee boy in 1950s' Glasgow with ferox fanaticism. The annals of angling were adorned with the works of men like T. Speedy, T.T. Stoddart, Osgood MacKenzie and W.C.G. St John, whose literary advocacy of ferox-fishing raised this branch of trout angling to that, in the status of Highland sport, of bagging a stag or salmon.

That status fell into disrepute in the years following the two world wars to be replaced by a derogatory bigotry associated with the 'effeminate' cult of fly fishing. Personally, I put this down to the use of pesticides, which had some negative effects on the male hormone production of Scottish manhood. Luckily for me, my grandfather had a plot (an allotment to 'sooth mooths') near Cathkin Park in Glasgow, where he believed in the organic production of fruit and flowers. This was long before Felicity Kendal made tight-fitting denims covered in dung look so enticing. My androgen supplies were thus saved from the debilitating delights of Iron Blue Duns and sunk nymphs. Unfortunately for me, they also caused a severe outbreak of plooks, which prevented me from testing my pubescent lust in the dance-halls of Glasgow. After finding that mammoths were extinct and having read about ferox, I decided to sublimate my unrequited desires in proving my manhood in the pursuit of this fish. I even took a job as a fisheries biologist to cover my true objectives. Thus began the first steps on that 'far cry' to Loch Awe and a British record trout.

Like all paths of true love, it was not a straight one, and it initially took me to Loch Quoich where, in June 1985, I teamed up with other guys also struck down by the charms of the 'ferox fatale'. This expedition proved that we had all been

Mr Thornton's house, with the red roof, where the barrage was built

Photo   *Malloch, Perth*

River Awe Salmon, 56 lbs.

Caught by Mr. H. G. Thornton, in "Pol Verie," on 12th June, 1923

H.B. Thornton's 56-pounder from the River Awe

Ailsa Craig and gannets in the mist

Neville filming on Jura; Mull is in the distance

The Paps of Jura

Casting lessons from the master: Arthur Oglesby

Belly-boating on Loch Dallas

The Storr Lochs below the Old Man of Storr

The Falls of Lealt

Evening on Loch Leven

The River Eden

taken for mugs by the elusive beast and we decided to combine efforts by forming the Ferox 85 Group. This is a sort of Lonely Hearts Club for anglers devoid of the company of 20-pound wild brown trout.

Organised on quasi-military lines, its rigorous induction and training regime soon weeds out the plankton-posers (people who fly fish), from those made of more relentless mettle. Those who survive this regime are graded into Ordinary Storm Troopers (Force 8–10 with driving sleet), and an unequalled ferox fighting force called the Special Relentless Squadron or SRS for short. Their names are now legends in at least one Pitlochry Street. Even Ballinluig has heard the stories of Aya Thorne, Pim Pirnie, Stevie Thorne, Burt Miller, Willie Ritchie and Ron 'The Hat' Greer.

Unknown to a beautiful and unsuspecting Argyll, this latter corps of dedicated dead-baiters was selected for a raid behind the barrage at the Pass of Brander in April 1993. Their mission, should they not self-destruct at the first pub, was to accept a chance to capture a new British record brown trout and lay forever the Ghost of Deviant Springs to rest. If you do not know the actual place I mean, good, you are still a real angler.

There were no refusals, even though preliminary annual sorties had proved the enemy elusive, environmental conditions harsh and billets brutal. Some mental scars from the most recent sortie were still unhealed, after the use of a caravan so compact and bijou that it still had the John West label on it. Luckily, an excellent beach-head position was discovered at Dalavich, in the form of the excellent facilities offered by the Forestry Commission holiday cabins. Their central location, licensed social centre and immediate juxtaposition to Norman Clark's boatyard, allow all regions of the loch to be reached in fighting condition. A premier piscatorial location, if ever there was one.

The SRS began operations at dusk on 17 April and maintained dawn o'clock to dark o'clock patrols for the subsequent week. Generally, this was technically successful but due to over-enthusiasm, they had to be guided home by Norman on one occasion. The following extracts from dispatches may be of historical interest to other anglers and of hysterical interest to those who took part:

DAY 1: Arrived in a single wave at 1630 hours. Morale was high and everyone full of relentless enthusiasm. This was quickly replaced by near mutiny when it was discovered that there was insufficient space in the refrigerator for both beer and dead-baits. Resolution of problem only came about by drinking the beer. Relentlessness thus happily restored. Kit inspection then carried out. Happily, bearing in mind the consumption of large amounts of baked beans in the NAAFI, chest-waders and all-in-one flotation suits came as standard. I expressed some concern about the large amounts of light ammunition in the personal ordnance supplies of individual troops. There seemed to be a surfeit of small Rapalas and other assorted lures more suitable for the capture of escapee rainbow trout from the internment camps of the aquaculture industry. The troops concerned denied this was the purpose of their ordnance choice and assured me it was only for the capture of fresh bait. There being insufficient evidence for a court-martial, I let the matter rest for the night.

DAY 2: Began field patrols after a full Scottish heart-attack breakfast with no bioflavenoids, vitamins, fibre or poly-unsaturates. Headed south-west in tight arrow-head formation. After only a few minutes, two platoons came under fire from several large escapee rainbows. These were horribly fat, flabby and finless, earning them the pejorative term 'schumbows'. The light ordnance had worked and my suspicions were once more aroused. I was highly sceptical of the frequent loud shout of 'Curses!' each time another schumbow was defeated. My platoon persisted with perfectly presented dead-baits for the duration of the day. The enemy, however, were well dug in and did not return our fire. Returned to base after ten hours rain-filled trolling. Ate eight schumbows.

DAY 3: Switched platoons and joined Pim Pirnie, resplendent in his bright red flotation suit. I'm sure it must have been a reject from a Noddy pantomime, but ferox are, thankfully, little concerned with sartorial elegance. We called him 'Big Red' because the hood hid his ears. I set up a three-quarter-pound sea trout on a wobble tackle and we headed south-west again. Nothing of account on outward patrol. Decided to investigate some shore-based attacks by auxiliary forces. These turned out to be 'Angling Ambassadors' from

Glasgow, replete with mandatory ancient blue Transit van and polythene bivvies. Their weaponry included bags of fish pellets to attract escapee schumbows. We wished them well in their attempt to follow in the footsteps of Walton and returned relentlessly to our battle. We were immediately engaged by an aquatic Panzer that fell for the sea-trout. A ten-minute exchange of fire resulted in the boating of an 8½-pound ferox. We knew it was a ferox even before this, for when it surfaced we could see fins on it. These fins were later the object of near-fatal astonishment to a passing Glasgow Ambassador who did not know that all fish were supposed to have them. An excellent day was rounded off with the appearance of reinforcements in the form of Dave Westwood with a bottle of Springbank malt. This is my next favourite whisky after Glen Horizontal. An excellent repast of ferox followed by detailed catch analysis.

DAY 4: A disgraceful day of unmitigated schumbow-bashing, worsened by the vandalism of my catch return by Aya Thorne and Big Red. They perceived this important document as either an ashtray or beermat rather than proof positive of personal piscatorial prowess. We repaired to the pub to repent and to renew our relentlessness.

DAY 5 and 6: Best taken together as the memory brings back horrible recollections of sodden hypothermia. It was fair to cry on Loch Awe. Highlights were limited to watching the snowline rise and fall on Ben Cruachan and the sleety rain fall not only on us but on the diaspora of English pike-anglers at Kilchurn. As we trolled towards the shore, many of them rushed out from their five-star brolly bivvies in anticipation of their 'satellite-tracking plonker-tronic fish-bite alarms' being set off. We reassured them we would be careful and admired the way they all looked identical to Kev, Trev and Nev from THE magazine. Aya defied providence by pouring a cup of water on his head to prove that we could not get any wetter. Headed north-east to the Pass of Brander. Our defeat here made that of John of Lorne's by Robert the Bruce look like a social-work problem. Fuel failures, engine fouling by set lines and having to be guided home by Norman Clark in the dark made the memories of past victory most distant.

DAY 7: Ferox, the Final Frontier; to Trollingly go beyond

400 rod-man hours. The dawn attack mounted by Big Red and Aya had failed. We joined them in support on an increasingly warm and pleasant day. Went west again, tooled up with heavy weapons in a last desperate bid to capture an enemy general. Looked bad by 1600 hours. Our smaller craft was running out of fuel and turned homewards. The unnamed brand of rod turned too, and the unnamed reel screamed a signal of which the British tackle industry has been so parsimonious in recognition. Only Partridge hooks vindicated their reputation. Relentlessness has its own reward, of course, and Aya Thorne and the Ferox 85 Group gained that in the form of a wild brown trout that initially tipped the scales at 20 pounds, but finally beat the official record by only a few ounces. We did this only by the timely intervention of boat-hirer Norman Clark and Christine Barret from the Oban Tourist Office who drove us, touching the ground no more than twice, to Taynuilt for weighing on accredited scales. [Echoes of Mr Thornton here.] After the epic, landing-net bending, 35-minute struggle with the fish, we were in no mood for a road race ourselves. This is the way to look after visitors. On our return, we just had time to phone the *Hooked on Scotland* team before our brains went into 'whisky neutral'. The programme we featured in later won the reward of a BAFTA award. To drink the drams of a dream come true on the shores of beautiful Loch Awe was indeed a fitting end to a fishing Odyssey. It is also a fresh beginning. We know there was a world record brown trout taken from Loch Awe in 1866 by W. Muir and his ghillie, Nicol McIntyre. This fish weighed 39 pounds 8 ounces, was taken with a trolled fly and, as it was hooked just outside the mouth, it was a record disallowed. As fisheries biologists, we know of no reason why there will not be another one. It is there for the taking by the relentless.

Argyll and Loch Awe, we will be back. See you on the shore, Paul, but can we have real glasses next time? Champagne in plastic cups? Really, Ricky!

After reading Ron's story, I have decided that from now on, I will know this wonderful water as 'LochmostsurprisingofAwe!'.

Chapter 13

THE RIVER CLYDE

A River Runs Pure Again

The shadowy figure crept along the side of the field, pausing for a moment to make sure that Prince was still quietly cropping the grass. Knife at the ready, the blond-haired man sidled up beside the Clydesdale and, in one deft movement – he'd done this before, obviously – cut a clump of hair from the horse's tail. Prince flinched briefly but relaxed as the man held a couple of sugar-lumps at the horse's muzzle. They were crunchingly accepted and then it carried on chewing a particularly sweet bit of grass.

The man made his way out of the field, clutching his prize. On the riverbank, he separated the precious strands and wound them into loops which he tucked safely into his tackle wallet. A satisfied grin spread over his face. Not for him the rigours of moistening silkworm gut until it was pliable, or the springiness of that new-fangled nylon. Clyde trout are shy and his father had found that horsehair casts were fine enough to fool the fish – and if they suited his father, a famous and revered Clyde fisher, well, they were good enough for him . . .

So might begin a romantic novel for Bills and Moon on the subject of tall, handsome Davie McCaster, the flaxen-haired, ripplingly muscled Clydesdale farmer who would rather spend his few spare hours in

125

pursuit of the trout of the Clyde than the valley girls, as the trout were more difficult to catch . . .

Well, perhaps not, but there are those who remember when the art of catching upper Clyde trout was almost entirely confined to the locals who knew the pellucid water well and *did* prefer fine horsehair to the coarse visibility of gut or nylon.

From its official source in the Lowther Hills near Leadhills, through Abington, Roberton, Symington and Thankerton to Lanark, the Clyde has some delicious trout water. The river is clear and the fishing difficult, but generations of resourceful local anglers have found ways to winkle out the trout, developing the flimsiest of flies and using natural baits like the gadger, the larva of the stonefly.

In 1887 a group of Clyde enthusiasts banded together to form the Upper Ward Angling Association to care for the fishing and husband the stock in the river. One man who worked tirelessly was Abington postmaster Matthew McKendrick, and his years of dedication were marked by the erection of a monument overlooking his beloved river just north of his home village. As well as fulsome praise as being a worthy man and a fine fisher, McKendrick has a delightful piece of homespun philosophy: 'Fish fair and free, and spare the wee anes.' We should all remember that.

Today, much of the fishing on upper Clyde is in the care of the United Clyde Angling Protection Association and I met former chairman William Miller beside part of that water. We were going to try the bait, Willie on the gadger or maggot, while I was looking forward to trundling a worm down some of the gravelly runs. I've always enjoyed worm fishing; perhaps it is the fact that the take is more prolonged – a knock, then a couple of ruggles, then nothing. You check your worm and see that something has chewed off the tail. A new one goes on and back out to the same place. The line lifts again and you tighten to feel the resistance of a wriggling fish; I love it. The first fish that took the worm was a small, beautifully coloured fish which followed McKendrick's advice and came off the hook before allowing anyone else to make the decision. They call these wee chaps 'Matta's bairns'. The next trout was more like one of Matta's teenagers. A gentle bite, or was it the bottom? No, it was a fish, a better one this time, difficult to judge the exact weight in the current, but in the net Willie was kind enough to give it just over the pound – a good fish and I was delighted. We put it back and it swam off, seemingly none the worse. Perhaps someday it will turn up as one of the 4-pounders that come off this part of the Clyde every year or two.

And we cannot leave Upper Clyde without mention of that other resident, the grayling. Reviled by some and revered by others, I have always considered this fish to be an asset to any river. I find it hard to agree with those who suggest that grayling damage stocks of other, supposedly more important, fish. Grayling have happily subsisted with salmon, trout and sea trout for many years in rivers like the Tay, Earn, Isla, Tweed and Teviot, all rivers with a high game fishing profile. Some keepers on these waters regarded the grayling as vermin and tried to net them out to reduce their numbers.

The Clyde fish were, it is said, introduced from Walton country, Derbyshire, last century and it was on the Clyde that the practice of winter grayling fishing in Scotland blossomed. Enthusiasm spread and groups of anglers would converge on the river on a crisp winter morning for a short day's sport. Certainly, the number of anglers grew mightily but there were many miles of water available, and as there was a tradition on the Clyde to keep fish caught, the grayling numbers were kept under control. Perhaps those keepers on the other rivers should have invited a party from Larkhall to fish for a day or two – the nets would never have been needed!

There has been a decline in stocks over recent years, not just because of angling. Abstraction, that invidious form of pollution, and many of the other pollutants that we know and hate in Scotland today are to blame. The reduction in water quality hits grayling hard. But one day, fishing fly at the tail of a pool, I rose dozens of tiny grayling, hooked a couple on a size-16 Greenwell nymph and was inwardly pleased that this 'Lady of the River' seems to be holding her own.

This is a lovely area to fish, and, with permits for both grayling and trout readily available for a modest price, it would be churlish to fish without making some contribution to the work started over a hundred years ago by Matthew McKendrick and his friends and nurtured since then by many Clyde devotees.

I'm not sure if there is any truth in the story that apprentices in Glasgow in the seventeenth century were guaranteed not to be given salmon more than three days a week, but there is a long history of salmon exploitation on the Clyde. From the twelfth to the fourteenth centuries, the monks of Paisley were granted various charters to net in the Clyde. In 1424 representatives of the Burghs of Renfrew and Dumbarton met at Old Kilpatrick (was it 'Old' even then?) to discuss their conflicting rights to certain salmon fishings – they were arguing about salmon even then! In the late 1700s there was an escalation in the rate of industrialisation and a rapid increase in population along the Clyde. By now, sewers were discharging directly into the river and water quality was diminishing. In 1869 salmon numbers above Glasgow were at a low level but poaching was still rife, one chap cleeking 14 fish from the River Nethan. In 1876 there was a Parliamentary report into pollution on the Clyde and its tributaries and from around 1900, though fish were still running the Leven and into Loch Lomond, the middle river was virtually dead.

Mike Shepley is a dreamer. He has had several dreams over the many years I've known him which have, in some way, come true. We used to have an occasional beer in the BBC Club in Botanic Crescent in Glasgow. The upstairs room looks over a leafily shaded part of that Clyde tributary, the Kelvin, just upstream of the graceful bridge which carries Queen Margaret Drive over the river. One day, Mike told me that he had dreamed of sitting in that room and seeing salmon splashing in the pool. 'Pshaw,' I said, 'that will never happen in our lifetime.' I take it back, Mike, because it has.

After that hundred years of industrial bashing, the middle section of the Clyde has healed. Not without help, mind you. Many interested bodies, not least the Clyde River Purification Board, have assisted in the recovery. Better sewage treatment and the decline in heavy industry brought an improvement in water quality. In 1983 fish were seen at Blantyre Weir for the first time in 80 years. The salmon were back in the Clyde and its tributaries.

So not only might Mike see fish in the Kelvin, he could fish for them. There is now a River Kelvin Angling Association and my 1994 membership card, number 30, tells me that there is a moratorium in force which deems that all sea trout and salmon caught should be carefully returned to the water. Brilliant. *I* must be dreaming. There was a unanimous vote from the members at the AGM to continue to return all fish, and a demand to send in a record of catches at the season's end and so help decide future stocking policy. We saw William Docherty take, photograph, of course, and return an autumn fish in the shadow of Kelvingrove Art Gallery and Museum. This is beyond even Mike's wildest dream.

Salmon which don't turn left into the Kelvin at Partick have a much harder time of it. Aiming upstream, there are spawning grounds on the

Avon, joining between Motherwell and Hamilton, the Nethan joining at Crossford, and other tributaries, and the farthest they could ever get on the Clyde would be to Stonebyres Falls. But the man-made weir at Blantyre, downstream of Bothwell Bridge, built in 1785 and heightened around 1850, is the major obstacle before the fish reach all that. Fish tend to congregate here, waiting for optimum water height before they can run over the weir. There are those who frequent this area who celebrate the return of salmon to the Clyde purely as a fiscal bonus. A fish caught represents money, and, as many people in the area are without work, who can blame them – though a twelve-year-old boy selling a lovely clean fish to a Chinese restaurant for a few pounds to buy cigarettes is less excusable. I wouldn't like to wade across the foot of the weir, though collectors of treble hooks would have a field day.

Fortunately, help is at hand. The River Clyde Fisheries Management Trust has been formed and the secretary, Jim McAloon, explained that the Trust had obtained a lease from Bothwell Bridge down to Erskine Bridge with a commitment to improve the fishing for the public good. The Trust has subleased the water from Bothwell Bridge to Dalmarnock Bridge to the Mid-Clyde Angling Association. It's £10 to join and £15 for the 1994 season, and according to the angling press in June, several sea trout have been taken, the best a 4-pounder and in late April a 12-pound salmon was landed. A late spring fish, this. Could the Clyde be developing a spring run? There are rumours of a big sea trout taken on the bend of the river near Celtic's football ground at Parkhead. Paradise indeed! And work is already under way on a fish pass at Blantyre Weir which it is hoped will be in operation at the end of 1994, allowing fish, shall we say, 'less-hindered' access to the spawning redds on the waters already mentioned. So hopes are high for a continued improvement in conditions for the fish (and, as a consequence, more fish) and we must support those who have done so much of the early, difficult work so unselfishly.

Sitting on the bank of the river below Dalmarnock Bridge, with scullers gliding over the surface of the water, I find it hard to think that salmon and sea trout are gliding past under it. But the coarse anglers have known for some time – these are not the silver fish they want at all. Steven McCaveney and Drew McCluskey are current Scottish Internationalists and Jim Brown is an ex-captain of the Scottish Coarse Fishing Team. This is a favourite part of the river on which to practise for matches, and apart from the dace and roach, perch and eels, sea trout

Shore fishing at Greenock

have been known to take a single maggot bait. Coarse anglers don't want them as they cannot be weighed-in for most competitions. Mind you, that wasn't the main problem for Jim that day. We met him in an earlier programme having a tuna, maggot and mud sandwich and in the interim, Jim, at the time a fishing-tackle shop-owner in Kirkintilloch, had occasion to get even closer to maggots. His giant maggot-cooling fridge broke down over a weekend, the temperature rose and the maggots woke up and got lively, as they say. When he and his wife opened the shop door it was 'Maggots from Hell'. One hundred and eighty gallons going walkabout. Three or four thousand in a pint, eight pints to the gallon – let's just say about five million. Three days sweeping up and three months suffering, as the ones they had missed decided to hatch: 'Bluebottles from Hell'. Jim is no longer a tackle shop-owner. But he still fishes, and with the maggot. No, that day Jim's problem was that, like so many Scottish footballers, he couldn't find the net. There were eels a-plenty being caught and I netted one for him, rather well if I may say so. Jim used the monofilament net to help him get a good hold of the fish and remove the hook without getting covered in eel slime. Instead of then putting it in the keep-net, he dropped it into the river. And he called *me* a jinx!

Drew was drawing fish to the net regularly on float, but Steven was fishing a swim feeder. He had been getting eels, too, and had taken a small dace when another bite moved the rod tip. It was a small brown trout, in excellent condition. As Steven returned it to the water, I felt a bit sorry for the coarse anglers, all these dashed game fish about. I made my escape downriver.

Doon the watter, actually, aboard the *Waverley*, bound for Rothesay. She's the last sea-going paddle steamer in the world, built in 1946 on the Clyde and it seemed only fitting that we should travel aboard her on our trip to Bute. From Anderston Quay, it was under the Erskine Bridge, past Dumbarton where the Leven joins from Loch Lomond, Greenock – all to the one side (port, actually) – Dunoon, Wemyss Bay, Inellan, round Toward Point and into Rothesay – a delightful journey and one made by tens of thousand of holidaymakers in the past. Would you believe we had a drop or two of rain at the beginning of our trip? I know it's unusual on a jaunt down the Clyde, but it is a great excuse to go below for a look at the engine: 2,100 horsepower, three cranks and a stroke of 66 inches, the largest ever fitted in a Clyde steamer. It is amazing the number of big wee boys who stand for ages watching this testament to Clyde engineering skills as it powers the *Waverley* through the water. Look through the portholes and see the 14-foot-diameter paddle wheels – it's always pretty wet in the paddle box. But approaching the pier, Bute was bathed in sun and we made for Loch Fad.

Bute is said to be the only Scottish island offering game, coarse and sea fishing. Loch Fad has wild brown and stocked rainbow trout; Quien high-quality but sometimes difficult brownies; Loch Ascog is famous for big pike and smaller perch; and Greenan Loch, stocked by the Isle of Bute Angling Club has carp, tench, bream and roach. You can shore fish near Rhubodach at the north end or Dunagoil Bay in the south for wrasse, pollack and cod, or try Kilchattan or Ettrick Bays for the flatties. That should be enough to keep you going.

To Fad we went, a fishery offering choice. Fly from a boat or bait from the bank. We opted for the boat with Alasdair MacFarlane, a keen fly fisher and committed Loch Fad fan. In 1992 Joe Bauld took a brownie of 7 pounds 8 ounces from Fad and there have been other fish over 6 pounds, well fed on the roach and perch in the loch, but it is the rainbows that are the main target. Reared in cages on the loch, they are acclimatised to the water, well conditioned and many overwinter, giving big fish every season. It's very pretty, too, the Sleeping Warrior on Arran framed by the trees on each side of the loch. Alasdair was soon into a fish on a Black Zonker. It was a bright day, so the best tactics were to fish below the surface, and the Zonker – a strip of rabbit fur with a gold bead at the head, fished on a sinking line – was the ideal lure. I weakened and tried the Zonker and got fish on it too. Lively and well marked, they were fine fish and a day on Fad is fun. On the way back, there were several groups of anglers who had made a day trip here from the Glasgow area and there is something a little exotic about taking a boat to an island for a day's fishing. And you can have a beer and a blether about the day as you go back up the watter.

The Clyde estuary south from Bute takes in the eastern side of Arran and widens to a natural geographic end on a line from Girvan to Ailsa Craig and the Mull of Kintyre – next stop, Northern Ireland. We all know how the sea fishing here has suffered over the last 20 or 30 years, how the runs of huge cod have disappeared and how there is hardly a haddock to be found from Glasgow to Girvan. But our journey down the Clyde from source to mouth would not be complete without a day at sea, and so it was that we loaded the gear aboard the *Rachael Clare* in Girvan harbour as skipper Tony Wass handed out the cups of tea. We made for Ailsa Craig, affectionately known as Paddy's Milestone because of its position roughly halfway between Glasgow and Belfast. A huge volcanic core over 1,000 feet high, it has long been famous for its large population of seabirds, notably the gannet colonies, and a quarry from which came the granite for the famous curling stones.

In under the cliffs on a day of sun and sea mist, I was amazed by the noise and the smell. Looking skywards, the birds were wheeling in and out of the mist swirling round the island and an umbrella might have been handy to avoid large amounts of what is sometimes known as 'good luck' landing on the old bunnet. We drifted close to shore and had coalfish, codling and some pollack, but Tony knew of a better mark south of Girvan so we headed for that.

A wreck in fairly shallow water, ideal for pollack. So what do we catch first? A good cod, about 10 pounds, for Stuart Smith. We tried ragworm bait, casting and retrieving – very exciting when you feel the fish take. But I kept striking the first bite when the fish took the tail of the rag rather than waiting until it had the whole worm and dived for cover – difficult not to, though. I did hook one good fish that seemed to wedge itself in the reef, but with a wee bit of luck I managed to boat it. There was a slash of colour on its side where it had been wedged in the rock, and I was lucky to land a fine 5-pounder. Big predator's mouth and sea-lice on it, not dissimilar from those you find on salmon.

Next, a fresh-run Kelvin pollack? If Mike dreams about it, you just never know!

Chapter 14

ISLAY AND JURA

Paps, Pollack and Port Charlotte

On a dark, late-autumn night, a young chap was cycling from Bowmore back to the Air Force Direction-Finding Base at Glenegedale. A car with lights blacked out came round a corner towards him and edged him into a ditch. He sat there dazed for a moment, then felt a warm liquid gently oozing down his leg. 'I hope it is blood,' he thought, having just bought, at great personal expense, and after considerable individual machination, a bottle of that most scarce resource, malt whisky. It may seem odd to call malt whisky on Islay scarce, but this was in 1943, wartime, and whisky *was* scarce. Unfortunately for this young man, he was unhurt; it wasn't blood and the liquid gurgling gently back into the very peat that made it taste so special was his precious whisky. Tragedy indeed. That young man was my father, doing his bit for the war effort, so my connection with Islay goes back a long way – just before I was born, in fact.

To make our programme, we had sailed from Oban on a day of bright sunshine, between Kerrera and the mainland, down the Firth of Lorne, with the Ross of Mull out to starboard and Scarba to port, then between Colonsay and the west coast of Jura and into Port Askaig. Our base was at Machrie, right beside Glenegedale, and as we made the journey towards Bowmore and on to fish Loch Gorm, I felt an empathy with this particular stretch of road and wondered which specific peat-hag had been the recipient of the contents of that priceless bottle on the fateful night.

We got to the lochside safely and met up with 'Billy the Butcher', Billy MacFarlane, a man who knows the loch well. Loch Gorm, the largest of Islay's fresh-water lochs, is fairly exposed, lying to the north of the Rhinns of Islay on the west coast of the island. Since the best fishing on the day of our visit was, as the wind decreed, well away from where the boats were stationed, elbow-grease was necessary in copious quantities. Great exercise, rowing. It was bright and sunny, not ideal, but Billy was hopeful. I fished with my favourite hairies: a hopper on the bob, a Soldier Palmer, and something dark on the tail, a Connemara Black. Gorm gives good fish every season with a pleasing average weight. Several fish made strenuous efforts to take our offerings, some succeeded and we landed a couple. Glinting in the sun, beautifully marked, spots everywhere, they typified wild Scottish brownies.

As did those from Loch Ballygrant. Donald James MacPhee, head keeper on Dunlossit Estate, eased the boat past the point and into Pounder Bay. It was a beautiful evening, and small fish had been turning at the fly with great regularity. More like the Bay of Plenty, in fact. Donald James reckoned that a bigger fish might take in the bay, but it was as we were returning to the boathouse in the dusk that the best fish came to the Connemara Black. Why did that fish not know that this is an Irish fly, tied originally to catch Irish fish? A lively 10-ouncer, slipped back into the water, the perfect end to a lovely night.

Next day, Donald James took me for a wander and we came to a small water covered in lily pads, the Lily Loch, would you believe. We were hoping to solve a wee bit of a mystery. Fish have been caught there which haven't been positively identified. Donald James reckoned them to be either roach or rudd, probably introduced years ago, and we tried like crazy to catch one, but the single maggot found favour with the trout rather than the mystery fish, so we left not knowing what they are. But I'd love to go back and find out the secret.

On the shore of another loch, just across the Port Askaig to Bowmore road from Loch Ballygrant, lies evidence that five or six hundred years ago those who fished on Islay did so with much more serious intent. The castle on Loch Finlaggan, now a site of national and historic interest, has been identified as the ancient seat and parliament of the Lords of the Isles. Many interesting artefacts have been found and the archaeologists working at the site now have a much clearer picture of how these people lived. Among pot shards and animal bones, they found some fish hooks. For environmental archaeologist and angler Mike Cressey, it was a most interesting find. The hooks are made of wrought iron and fashioned to the same design as the modern eyeless hook, though much cruder, but with a barb and a spade end for taking the line. They have been dated back to around 1400 and, because of their size, I'd imagine they were used at sea rather than for trout. There is certainly evidence that these people travelled to the coast, in that various seashells have been found, including a cache of limpets. Somehow 'Limpet Stew' does not make the mouth water in the way that 'Steamed Mussels' does, but perhaps limpets tasted better in the fifteenth century. All the finds here are being collated and taken to the museums of Scotland to give a broader picture of the history of the island. It is a fascinating and atmospheric spot for anyone interested in Scotland's past, with the added advantage that permits are available to fish the loch.

Other than Finlaggan, Islay has plenty to see and do on the non-fishing days. A great place for bird-watchers, it is another of the few places where the corncrake's crackle can be heard. And that master of aerobatics, the chough, finds Islay to its liking. This member of the crow family, disappearing fast from many parts of the country, can still be seen

Loch Finlaggan – home of the Lords of the Isles and ancient fish hooks

137

near mountain, crag and cliff, wheeling and soaring and gliding and diving on broad, rounded wings, the tips spread like fingers and all the time giving free rein to its musical *keeaar* call. The Mull of Oa in the south is one place to go with binoculars for a sight of this interesting bird, easily distinguished from other members of the crow family by its purple-black glossy plumage, red legs and curved red bill.

Islay has for a long time been a winter home to large numbers of geese. The birds like it here and always have done – conditions suit them. The island has always had limited shooting and, as Dr Malcolm Ogilvie told me, there are no foxes, no badgers and no moles to give the birds problems. From roughly mid-October to mid-April, thousands of bar-nacle and white-fronted geese hone in on the farmers' fields. These birds breed in Greenland in summer, but about 65 per cent of the barnacles and 30 per cent of the white-fronts come to winter on Islay. This causes problems for the farmers as the birds are very keen on grass, preferably the newly sown bright green stuff. Unfortunately, because it is rich in nutrients, that is the very grass the farmers would like to feed to their cattle or sheep. Conflict. Realising that the farmers do have a case, Scottish Natural Heritage pays the farmers a sum every year to com-pensate for grass taken by the geese. Nonetheless, if you want to see numbers of these large birds, try wintry Islay.

There is the Museum of Islay Life in Port Charlotte, where a visit gives another insight into the way people have lived on the island throughout the years. Bowmore Church, standing at the top of the village, is unusual in being round – no corners for the devil to hide in; an imposing building looking down the main street towards the pier where scenes for that wonderful film, *The Maggie,* were shot. There are walks of interest all over the island. Although only about 30 miles across, Islay has more than 130 miles of coastline, some parts with steep cliffs and rocky inlets, others with golden sand with no one but yourself to savour it, and if the sea is a trifle cool for bathing, pop into the Mactaggart Pool in Bowmore for a relaxing swim or invigorating sauna.

Then there are the distilleries, of which Islay has more per square mile than any other part of Scotland. The names, apart from being famous the world over, are delightful, amongst them Caol Ila, Bruichladdich, Bunnahabhain, Lagavulin and Laphroaig. My father knew of their existence that dark night so long ago, but was probably not aware of how the mystical product was conjured from a simple mix of prime barley steeped in pure Islay water, malted and dried over the

smoke from a swirling fire of Islay peat, so absorbing the famous 'peat-reek', and then mashed with yeast and more Islay water for fermentation to take place in large vats. This cloudy brew is then given over to the skill of the stillman who watches over the first distillation in those beautiful swan-necked copper stills, and takes the prime cut of the second distillation to store in oak sherry or bourbon casks for ten or more years to allow a fusion of the ingredients and the salty air of Islay to work its magic. Nowadays, most distilleries are delighted to welcome visitors, as we were at Laphroaig, just outside Port Ellen in the south of the island, explain the process and perhaps even give a taste of the end product before you leave. Just the job to gee you up for another day on the water.

Mind you, if you have a day out with Tony Dance, the Pavarotti of Port Charlotte, his operatic renderings will be more than enough to gee you up without recourse to Islay malt. Tony is a big chap, with a big heart and a wonderful voice. That voice is heavily tinged with the accent of the west country – he came to Islay on holiday, loved the place and the people, upped sticks and is now a guest-house owner and sea fishing boat-hirer. The sight of two killer whales, male and female, spouting not

The round church at Bowmore – 'with no corners for the Devil to hide in'

a hundred yards from his boat, the sunsets and the peace and tranquillity have converted him into an Islay-lover. We sped out from Port Charlotte on a bright, sunny evening across Loch Indaal, bumping across the waves to the submerged reef at Laggan Point. Fleets of gaudy flies pulled saithe – the coalfish – to the surface, grey and olivey; and pollack, whose colours reflected the rich brown of the kelp from which they'd been drawn. One or two were kept for the folks in the village, both fish being a tasty table treat when prepared shortly after capture. The sun was dancing on the western horizon as we made for home and Tony gave us another operatic rendition – an adaptation of 'The Pearl Fishers' – 'The Pollack Fishers'.

Had we been a boat, fishing for our livelihood, we might have had to make an equitable share of what we had taken. In the past, there was a tradition in Scotland that all sea fishers share the catch in a way that favours no individual. The method is simple. One share is given to the boat and one to each member of the crew. If there were four men fishing, there would be five shares. The catch would then be divided by the fishermen as equally as possible into five piles on the pier. Each man would then take a stone, marking its own particular characteristics, and place it in the middle of the shares of fish. A stranger, not knowing to whom the stones belonged, would then be called upon to pick them up and lay a stone beside each share, every man of the crew taking the share alloted by his stone. Because no one knew which pile of fish they might be allotted, they would have made the original division of the catch as fair as possible. An honest way to conduct business, the principle of which, if applied by modern business, might bring some honour to certain sections of the mercantile community.

There is a growing band of anglers on Islay who enjoy a day fishing from the shore, and large parts of the coastline offer the chance to try for a variety of species. I'm sure there must be a beach or two suitable for bass fishing, the bass being a fairly new phenomenon in many parts of Scotland. And there is a chance to take sea trout in salt water at Loch Gruinart. I tried for an hour or two, had a tiny finnock and rose one good fish. It is a delight to fish between the seaweed-covered boulders and the patches of golden sand. There were seals about, but we did see one or two good sea trout leap clear of the water. With the right tides and a bit of local knowlege, I'll bet some anglers have had a day to remember here.

From many parts of Islay, you might be forgiven for thinking that the island is fairly mountainous, but the highest point, Beinn Bheigeir, at

Machair bay, Islay

1,609 feet is almost 1,000 feet lower than what you are probably seeing, the Paps of Jura. The three mountains are all over 2,400 feet, with Beinn an Oir not far short of a Munro at 2,571 feet. The short ferry journey from Port Askaig to Faolin takes you onto the only main road on Jura, winding round the southern shore and up the east coast before petering out north of Ardlussa pier 24 miles later. Jura is another naturalists' paradise, over 100 species of birds having been seen there. There are around 20 deer on the hills to each of the 250 inhabitants, making deer-stalking an important element in Jura's life. The hills are also home to some delightful trout lochs and we met up with head keeper John Connor near Tarbert for the first stage of our journey to try to tempt a trout or two.

We boarded a small boat in Loch Tarbert which took us out to a larger cruiser. With the rowing-boat in tow, a delightful sail through the narrows brought us to the wider part of the loch where we got back into the wee boat and headed for a deserted sandy beach. The water was crystal clear, the sky a vivid blue except where the vapour trails of two jets painted a St Andrew's Cross at 35,000 feet. The next stage was by hill vehicle and as we clambered aboard, John's dog, Tess, was having the time of her life. We set off up the side of a small burn and after breasting a couple of rises, the views started to unfold. Small lochs lay to our right in folds of hill and as we climbed higher, the panorama broadened. The views were stunning. Down over the raised beaches, the surf pounded the rocky shore, Colonsay sat starkly in the blue sea and the outline of Mull shimmered in the distance.

Deer were watching us curiously as we made our way to a loch near the shore. Tess suddenly found something of interest in the tufts of grass and John had to call her to heel before she thought the gull chicks in the many nests were something to play with. The bright sunshine made fishing difficult, but a willing brownie took the Invicta and came splashing to the bank. The fish in these lochs are not big, typical hill-loch size, but there are plenty of them and some of the parties that come for a few days can take several hundred. Most are returned, though there are those who say that reducing the numbers might increase the average size. But for me, the great thing about my day was the journey – the boat from Islay, the drive to Tarbert with superb views over the Sound of Jura to Kintyre and Knapdale, the other boats and the hill vehicle. You know that not many people get the chance to visit such a beautiful spot, and that heightens the fishing pleasure. On the journey back, we stopped for a last cast or two on the last loch and a golden brownie set the seal on a day that will live in the memory.

Talking of seals, one popped its head out of the water to take a closer look at me as I stood at the most northerly tip of Jura. The tide was moving swiftly between me and the island of Scarba – I was looking out over the notorious Strait or Gulf of Corryvreckan – and I was casting into slack water in the hope of a coalie or pollack. The seal and a number of his pals had been snooping round since we arrived, so I imagine the fish were keeping their heads well down in the kelp. The tide was now making a fair old rate of knots, causing waves to form over a reef on the Scarba side of the channel. They say that when the tides are at their fiercest here, a whirlpool is formed and you can hear the boiling sound at some distance. A place to be avoided by small craft, but one where a young Scandinavian prince was asked to prove his love for the daughter of one of the Lords of the Isles. Breackan had asked for her hand in marriage and her father agreed, on condition that he spend three days and three nights out on the whirlpool to show his bravery. Breackan agreed and returned home, where he had three ropes spun; one of hemp, one of wool and one of maidens' hair, as he knew the purity and innocence of the maidens would give it extra strength. Back he came, went out into the whirlpool and anchored his boat. On the first day the tide was strong enough to break the rope of hemp, on the second it was too much for the rope of wool, but on the third all was going well until, just before dark, the rope of maidens' hair parted. One of the maidens who had given her hair wasn't a maiden at all and of course the rope lost its strength. Poor old Breackan was drowned, though his body was washed ashore and dragged by his faithful dog to a cave – Breackan's Cave. And that is the end of the legend of Breackan. Or is it? Many years later, a stone coffin was found in a cave near the area. I think it would be nice if the coffin was Breackan's and he had been laid to rest near where he died to prove his love of a Scottish princess.

Another who had experience of the whirlpool was the writer George Orwell, who came to live on Jura in 1946. He set up home at Barnhill, a fairly remote farmhouse near the northern end of the island. He was not a well man but he loved Jura; in 1947 he gave up his cottage in Hertfordshire and the following year did not renew the lease on his London flat, intending to make Jura his only home. He had a boat and loved going round to the west coast through the Gulf of Corryvreckan. On one of these trips, the boat was caught in the whirlpool, where the engine fell off and the boat turned upside-down nearby one of the islands in the Strait. All those aboard managed to reach the island, but had to stay there until they were picked up by a fishing boat. Orwell wrote his most famous book at Barnhill, but had difficulty in finding a title, thinking of calling it *The Last Man in Europe*. The book was completed in 1948, so eventually he changed the last two numbers round and thus we got *1984*.

Like so many rivers on the western side of Scotland, those on Islay need rain for the salmon fishing. It had been fairly dry for some time as we headed for the upper part of the River Laggan, but there had been a bit of water a few days earlier. Dunlossit Estate has this fishing and Donald James MacPhee had suggested there might be a fish or two in the pools. The river is pretty small here, well above the back road from Bridgend to Port Ellen, but that means you've got to fish light. The trout rod will do fine, a floating line and 6- or 8-pound nylon. I fished a wee Silver Stoat dropper and that wonder from Mr Gowans, Ally's Shrimp. There were one or two little riffles that looked fishy and at one I saw what I thought might be a sea trout head and tail. A couple of casts later, a fish hit me with a terrible thump and shot off downstream. I followed it, still thinking it might be that sea trout but it was, wonder of wonders, a salmon. I was fishing unencumbered, just the wellies, a spool of nylon in my pocket, a fly or two in the hat and, once again, no net. The bank was quite high so I had to lead the fish upstream towards a shingly bay. I was trembling with excitement, as I had barely expected to *see* a fish, far less hook one. Luck was on my side, though, as I managed, rather untidily, to slip a finger under its chin and land it; a small, slightly coloured late-summer fish around 5 pounds. The fact that the dropper was firmly snagged in my jumper is perhaps proof that greedily trying to fish two flies may bring a downfall, as that fly could just as easily have caught on something in the river and the fish would have been gone. On the other hand, I had actually caught two things – a salmon and myself!

Time to celebrate with a dram, I thought, then remembered my father and the trouble to which he had gone in 1943 to acquire such a luxury. It didn't seem right to open the hip flask and simply have a dram in the open air. But I did!

Chapter 15

SPEYSIDE

Whisky Runs Through It

'I know the spring catches made on these waters in recent seasons, but as I have no special permission to mention them, I do not give them. But, dear reader, if you can afford the rent and if you get the chance for February, March, April and May, let me urge you to ask no questions but jump at it blindfold. You will not regret it.'

Our old friend Augustus Grimble, writing about the River Spey before the First World War, and for a man who had fished most of the great rivers at the best times of the year, that was praise indeed, and the fishing must have been pretty good. These were the days when the Spey spawning beds were counted each season. The number varied between 5,500 and 7,500 and it was calculated that over 120,000,000 eggs might be deposited in the redds. Grimble observes that these were not just scrapes and shallow depressions: 'Plenty of them would make a burial place for a dead sheep and I have seen a few that would serve the same purpose for a donkey!'

But all was not sweetness and light. The Spey suffered badly from the discharge of 'burnt ale' coming from the many distilleries which had recently appeared on its banks. This noxious liquid was deadly to parr, fry and smolts while sickening any salmon in the vicinity. The discharge turned the water into a muddy yellow colour with froth on the surface and, of course, fishing prospects vanished. The distillers were obstinate about their right to foul the river in this manner and it eventually took a successful court action by the Countess Dowager of Seafield on behalf of the proprietors to change their minds.

The Spey is a river that I have not often fished and do not know well, much to my regret, and these snippets from the past help me to get the present into proportion. When we arrived at the old bridge over the Spey near Grantown to talk to Arthur Oglesby about his fishing course (and his photograph of Grace on Loch Voshmid!), it was interesting to cast my mind back to Grimble's days.

Mind you, casting has always featured in my life. As an actor, I hope to be cast in some interesting and challenging work and as an angler, I hope that no one will copy all the bad casting habits I've learned. I find it surprising that some people will spend a fortune on a week's fishing, a similar amount on tackle of the highest quality and then happily trundle off with no idea how to use it, unwilling to spend a few quid on casting lessons. Bad casting shows, whether on the riverbank or television.

For almost 30 years, Arthur has been hosting fishing courses at Grantown-on-Spey, with an emphasis on casting. With him, many people from all walks of life have discovered the pleasure to be derived from conscious control of rod and line and an appreciation of the special qualities of Speyside and its fishing. Arthur is no martinet; he saw I was able to put a fly out in a somewhat unconventional way and I was delighted to hear him say that the whole purpose of casting was just that – to get the fly out. But if pushed, he will extol the virtues of (guess what) the Spey Cast. It is difficult to explain the nuances on paper, but watching Arthur do it on water, it looks so easy. Try it, with phrases like: 'Draw a big crescent moon in the sky with the rod point . . . slow lift, crescent moon and punch it out . . . try to break the rod in that final push, talk to the reel, as if it was a microphone beside your face.' It is very difficult to unlearn bad habits, but if you come to Arthur with none, you may leave with some good ones.

Like the habit of catching fish. Arthur had organised a day on one of the Castle Grant beats and as we walked down the riverbank, I could see why people come back every year. Absolutely fabulous fly water. Beautiful popply streams where the fly worked a treat. Lionel Main, our excellent ghillie, kept me right on all the details: where to start, how deep to wade, what length of line to fish; and the excitement, the thrill of fishing such wonderful water, was heightened by the sight of salmon

heading and tailing further down the pool. On a new bit of water, I always find myself asking the ghillie where a fish might take – until you actually move one yourself, the pool remains a mystery, even though you are told that fish can take anywhere. Lionel was very patient, assuring me I was doing all right. Of course, by now I had reverted to my old casting methods and soon hooked a tree on the backcast. I wasn't the first ever to do that, though, Lionel told me as he shinned up the tree to retrieve my fly – the Tarzan of Castle Grant! We heard a shout from upstream and saw Arthur into a fish. Second time down the Croy Race he hooked a lively salmon on a size 8 Blue Charm. The charm worked and a late-spring fish of about 9 pounds slid into the net, one small sea-louse on the gill-cover indicating its freshness. Arthur made it all look so effortless, another good habit to learn.

The Speyside railway

I fished on and moved two salmon, without touching either – another bad habit to be avoided if possible. But the day wasn't over yet. As evening approached, tackle and tactics were changed to meet the challenge of that wily powerhouse of silver, the sea trout. The Spey has long been famous for its sea trout fishing and few rivers can rival the quality of the fishing here. And not just on the exclusive beats either. The Strathspey Angling Improvement Association controls around seven miles of excellent water (roughly from Nethy Bridge to a mile below the Old Spey Bridge and about 12 miles of the River Dulnain), surely some of the best Association water in the country, and weekly tickets can be had for fairly modest outlay.

As the gloaming settled, we could hear them. Sea trout are usually fairly quiet in daylight hours, but now they were active, boiling and splashing at the tail of the pool. I managed to get a finnock of about a pound before darkness proper fell and the river changed character. Night fishing is like being in another world. The sounds of nature seem to tell different stories than in daylight . . . a pipistrelle bat flitting past can mutate in the mind. You are fishing by feel, wondering if the cast is tangled, if you are reaching that ideal spot under the trees on the far bank, all the time trying to wade as gently as possible, making as little disturbance as you can. It is a fascinating way to fish and your nerves are crackling with expectancy. When a fish takes, and it can be gentle or with a clatter, all that tension is released as you try to work out how big the fish is and where the heck it is off to! Sometimes the only way of knowing is to look at the rod top against the night sky. You have to be careful netting fish at night, too – the dropper can catch the net or the tail fly snag a rock and your hard-earned fish will be gone. The fish I got was not big, a couple of pounds or so, but a glistening silver sea trout nestling nocturnally in the net was ample reward for a long Spey day.

Actually, on Speyside there are many ways to spend your days. One brochure lists three interesting churches to visit, eleven ancient monuments or antiquities, five museums, battlefields and galleries, thirteen visitor centres and entertainments, seven wildlife and nature reserves, three gardens and garden centres, two watersports centres, six golf courses, six pony-trekking and riding centres and even, in this cradle of Scottish mountain skiing, several dry-ski slopes.

From where the River Truim, formed at Dalwhinnie, joins the Spey near Cluny's Cave above Newtonmore all the way to Grantown and beyond, there is not a day of the year when you can find an excuse to be idle. Landmark Highland Heritage and Adventure Park at Carrbridge is one of the busiest attractions. Set in an ancient Scots Pine wood, the focus is on just that: wood and forestry. Ruthven Barracks, the last retreat of the followers of Bonnie Prince Charlie, and the Highland Folk

Museum in Kingussie bring history to life. Wildlife – the area is rich in it. The Cairngorm Reindeer Centre near Aviemore has Britain's only herd and the 260-acre Highland Wildlife Park at Kincraig allows you to get close to wild horses, red deer and bison, red fox, wildcat and otter. Crossbills and crested tits, the capercaillie and the osprey can all be seen in the Speyside pinewoods, the ospreys rearing their chicks on the RSPB site at Loch Garten being one of the most popular visitor attractions. Or try the Speyside Steam Railway, chuffing happily between Boat of Garten and Aviemore, nostalgically summoning up times past. And Speyside is synonymous with whisky. There is a malt whisky trail taking in famous names like the Glenlivet, Glenfiddich and Glen Grant, and the new Speyside Cooperage visitor centre at Craigellachie shows all about the ancient craft of barrel-making in the 'Acorn to Cask' exhibition.

In the Cairngorms lies the largest area of high ground in Scotland, with Ben Macdhui (the second-highest of the Scottish mountains), Braeriach, Cairn Toul and Cairn Gorm all over 4,000 feet. Winter sports

Speyside reindeer

feature here, with skiing and climbing and hill-walking bringing thousands of people to enjoy the exhilaration of the mountains. From Cairn Gorm you can look down to Loch Avon or Loch A'an, from Beinn Mheadoin you can see Loch Etchachan at a height of over 3,000 feet and frozen over for many months of the year, and the panorama to the north-west reveals many lower-lying waters of interest to the trout angler.

On another sunny day we fished Loch Vaa, beautifully set in the pinewoods near Boat of Garten, the name referring to the ferry that existed here before the road bridge was built over the Spey. This loch is crystal clear and stocked with rainbows to supplement the natural brown trout population. Easing out from the boathouse, I could see it wasn't going to be easy to fool a fish in the sunshine, but I had confidence, as Lionel Main was my ghillie again, and once more I relied on a trusty cast of hairy flies to attract the trout. There was a brisk breeze, and as Lionel held the boat off the rocky points, good fish came to the fly. It is a wonderful, if frustrating, sight to see large trout flatten the wave as they turn and miss the fly, but eventually one took hold and I was playing an acrobatic rainbow as powerful as any I have had of that size. Over 2 pounds, Lionel and I thought, it was just reward for good teamwork.

There are trout to be had from waters throughout Speyside and char from Loch Insh near Kincraig. This is a water that caters for canoeing, windsurfing, sailing and angling – there is room enough for everyone. Dick Carr had gone so far as to catch some char. He had been trolling for salmon with a two-inch black and gold Devon Minnow, well weighted to get it down to, say, 15 feet. His fish were spade-tailed and handsome, with white piping on the fins. Many years ago, Dick caught two char from Loch Insh over 4 pounds on the same day. He wasn't sure what they were at the time. He knows now, though – British records, that's what they were.

So, Speyside is full of surprises. I was certainly surprised when Ricky told me to be ready to meet Grant Mortimer, who owns the excellent tackle shop in Grantown, as we were going to fish American-style at Dallas. I jumped into the Range-Rover and Grant offered me a Barbour stetson in exchange for the bunnet and we were on our way to Dallas. We passed some big ranches and mighty fine country on our way, I thought, to the airport, but at a junction we took the south fork and my dreams of fishing with J.R. were dashed. Certainly we were at Dallas – Loch Dallas near Auchgourish, via Boat of Garten – and the 'American-style' was a belly-boat, float-tubing, call it what you will. Complete with chest-waders and flippers, I sat myself into this American innovation and pushed off from the shore. It was delightful, like fishing from your own personal armchair. You have total control over where you go on the water – if you see a fish rising you can, with a swish or two of the flippers, get within casting range and hold yourself there.

But this is not a casual item. It has safety chambers and all kinds of straps and devices to keep you safe, and an inflatable life-jacket should be worn at all times. It is for small, still waters – not to be recommended for rivers or large lochs where weather can change suddenly, and never to be used alone. Safety first, remember.

Dallas is another loch with brown and rainbow trout and as I gently propelled myself past a pair of mildly surprised ducks, I saw a good fish rise. The fly went out, the fish came up and I was into a good rainbow, I thought, except it was a brown trout. When will I ever learn? The great thing about this method is that you are virtually at loch level and I brought the fish gently onto the fitted apron stretched across the front of the belly-boat. It is handy for keeping your fly-line neat as you retrieve and is also marked with an inch rule. As the trout was lifted aboard and measured at 15 inches, it was a simple job to show it to the camera, unhook it and plop it back into Loch Dallas.

The belly-boat has clips for a landing net and numerous pockets for your gear. Or whatever. I am partial to a beer now and again and unbe-known to Ricky and Neville, I had sneaked a glass and a can of Export aboard. You see, another great thing about fishing this way is that you can declare the bar to be open when you want. As the fish went back, I felt justified in declaring it open, opened the pocket, opened the can and paddled off into the Dallas sunset, happier than J.R. and his cohorts had ever been.

The Texan Dallas might have captivated millions over the years, but to be afloat in a belly-boat on the Speyside Dallas on a summer evening, beer in one hand, rod in the other, well, I certainly didn't care who shot J.R. Ewing. You have to get your priorities right!

Chapter 16

SKYE

High, Dry and Fish on the Fly

The Old Man of Storr was wreathed in mist and the Old Man of *Hooked on Scotland* was wreathed in smiles. I was about to fish the Storr Lochs once again. I had last fished these lovely waters in 1988 on a mild May evening. We had been filming Douglas MacKinnon's graduation film, *Ashes* and that day I had finished just after lunch, bought a permit in Portree and taken the boat out from the bay by the road. I had arranged to meet Alec Heggie, one of the other actors, when he finished working, so I was alone in the boat with a pork pie and a can of beer. It was a perfect afternoon and I drifted along the shore, watching a redshank work the line between peat and sand. There were trout rising, I caught a few and it seemed only minutes before Alec arrived. That is the thing about Skye. It is a great time-consumer, in the best possible way. After he arrived, we caught some more fish and, whenever we meet, we still talk about it as a wonderful night.

So, I was glad to be back, fishing this time with Dr Calum MacRae, recently retired and a Storr Lochs expert. A bit of a character is Calum, and a very popular member of the Skye Angling Association. He came to Skye for a month in 1957 and stayed. I asked him what flies he was going to use and he wasn't too forthcoming, referring to them simply as his 'secret weapons'. I fancied a fairly traditional cast, with a daddy-style

With Dr Calum Macrae at the Storr Lochs – secret weapons have done the trick!

bob fly, a Kate McLaren and an Invicta – hardly secret weapons, and well proven in tactical warfare against Scottish trout.

Although the Old Man was invisible in the mist, conditions were not too bad, just enough of a breeze to give a decent fishing wave.

The two lochs, Leathan and Fada, produce fish that average about three-quarters to a pound and every year some big fish are taken, usually from Leathan, up to 5, 6 and 7 pounds. Calum's secret weapons and my overt ones were working well and it was only when I netted a fish for Calum that I realised he was fishing *four* flies – the devious Doctor had not told me! Not only that, I was netting fish for him left, right and centre. Just a dogsbody, me. But I had one or two myself, including a fish over a pound just at the end of the evening. Calum was great company and I have now had two memorable outings for the trout of the Storr Lochs.

That night, we had visual proof of why Skye is known as 'Eilan a' Cheo', the Misty Isle, but it is not always like that. A blink of sunshine on the hills and you can see why this, the largest of the Scottish islands, has captivated the hearts of so many visitors.

The Cuillin Hills are surely the most precipitous in the country, grouped together at the south of the central part of Skye. There are around 15 peaks over 3,000 feet, some of them having only been conquered at the end of last century, long after most of the Alps had been climbed, and still a real challenge to the most skilled climbers. The Black Cuillins form the main ridge, with the Red Cuillins round Loch Coruisk to the south. Though beautiful, the mountains can be dangerous and great care should be taken by anyone thinking of climbing there.

And north-east Skye, Trotternish, has a complex and varied geology. Fossil remains, such as the fish-lizard, Ichthyosaurus, and dinosaur footprints have been found at Bearreraig Bay below the Storr Lochs, and at Valtos, between Lealt and Mealt. They are over a hundred million years old. And it is not difficult to imagine the volcanic upheaval that produced the pinnacles and gullies of the Quiraing – the Table, the Needle and the Prison – hiding-places in the past for stolen cattle.

All this high ground is, of course, the birthplace of many burns, joining towards lower ground to form the few waters which have regular runs of salmon and sea trout. As is typical of west, these rivers tend to be of the spate variety, needing a good flush of water to make them darken the riverside stones and bring in the salmon. Likely rivers are the Sligachan, the Hinnisdale and the Snizort.

The upper Snizort is really bonny. Rocky falls and deep pools are just ideal for the worm, and as you drop the bait into the peaty depths you have that wonderful feeling of having a tangible contact with the unknown. The line follows the river's course and then stops briefly. It moves sideways and you can actually *feel* there is something at the other end. It is not always possible at that point to detect the size of the fish so there is again a delicious expectancy waiting to be realised. Of course, this moment can resolve itself in a number of ways:

(1) You wait for ages for the bite to develop, it doesn't, you tighten and there is nothing there.
(2) You wait for a little while for the bite to develop, it doesn't, you tighten and there is nothing there.
(3) You panic at the first sensation of a touch, strike like mad, thinking 'this is a salmon', and a six-inch trout comes out of the pool and over your head, probably the first ever from that pool to experience the dubious delights of air travel.

It wasn't quite that bad, but I did hope the bite that made the line rattle so well might just have been from a bigger fish, but no. This was a sunbed fish, tanned the colour of Pete. He was just back from six weeks on the Costa Fortune, and was the colour of peat. It was thin, too, showing that there is not a lot of natural feeding in the upper reaches of these rivers and maybe that's why fish went to sea to feed in the first place. But back it went and we moved downriver, to where the rocky hillsides gradually give way to rolling farmlands to meander slowly to the sea beside Skeabost House Hotel.

It is here you'll meet Stuart McClure, freelance ghillie and guide; a man who has known the river for many years and has gained a reputation for being a dab hand at worming out the odd salmon. On these lower reaches, he prefers to use a light spinning rod and reckons a Snizort salmon always takes the worm the same way, gently to begin with, then you'll feel a knock. You should give it time and be prepared for the fish to take you 10 or 15 feet downstream, knocking all the way, where it will stop and chew the worm. That is when Stuart tightens. I suppose the way a fish takes is dictated by the kind of water in which it is lying. I've had them go for a worm like a ton of bricks in rocky gullies and seen them ignore a bait twenty times in clear water only to take on the twenty-first.

Stuart was fishing a single shot with the worm, just enough to let it bounce along the bottom of the run into the pool. It was a nice high bank and he kept well back from the edge to avoid spooking the fish. We were getting bites almost immediately (the midges were out in force), but soon Stuart had the kind of bite we like. We knew there were salmon in the pool as we'd seen them moving, but this turned out to be a sea trout about a pound and a half, better than the normal finnock which average three-quarters. So, no Snizort salmon for us, but with water well worth worming, and there is good fly water too.

For me, part of the thrill of islands is the getting there. I love the boat trip across the water, the propellers churning the blue water into creamy foam astern, and the bow thrusting salty spray to port and starboard. And though the sail from Kyle of Lochalsh on the mainland to Kyleakin on Skye is only a matter of minutes, it's the principle that counts. You queue and wait your turn. You get onto the ferry, out of the car and up onto the deck. The vessel leaves the slip, you sniff the sea and it's back to the car for disembarking onto Skye. It will not be the same

The Skye ferry – I'll be sad to see it go

with the new bridge that is being built. It makes it too easy and I will not feel I've earned the right to be on the Island.

Many in the past have made the journey to Skye, for a variety of reasons. Dr Samuel Johnson and James Boswell came here in 1773 on their peregrinations round the Western Isles. Boswell made some interesting comments about the food available on Skye at the time. He says, 'At tables where a stranger was received, neither plenty nor delicacy was wanting.' There was much wild-fowl, and stag and roebuck, but no hare. Fish was plentiful and there was no lack of beef, sheep or goats. Native bread consisted of oat or barley cakes and wheat was used without yeast to make unfermented bread, seldom moulded into a loaf, but eaten as a cake. A gentleman's breakfast began with a dram and then might follow tea and coffee with butter, honey, jams and marmalades. 'If an epicure could remove by a wish, in quest of sensual gratifications, wherever he had supped, he would breakfast in Scotland.' Thank goodness we could do something right, though there was a down side. It seems that many houses piled the table high with large slices of Cheshire cheese, 'which mingles its less grateful odours with the fragrance of the tea'. The Doctor, more used to the manners of the south, was taken aback by the overt friendliness of his welcome. 'What is it to live and not to love?' exclaimed Mistress Mackinnon at Corriechatacan, as she embraced the Doctor's ample frame.

Many other visitors have had proof of the friendliness of the people, not least the MacLeods, whose roots reach deep into Skye. If you look at the shape of the island on a map, it seems to be stretching away from its brief contact with the mainland at Kyle, out towards the Uists, into the Atlantic and beyond. Which is where many islanders went over the years, for a variety of reasons, and when they return it might be to Dunvegan Castle, the home of MacLeod of MacLeod and Clan seat. With parts of the building dating back to the ninth century, it is the oldest castle in private hands to have been in continuous occupation by the same family. Inside, you can learn of the clan battles, the legends and tragedies, the murders and loves and romances which make up the history of the clan and the castle. Among the items on display are the two-handed sword of Rory Mor, the twelfth chief, the 'Fairy Flag' reputed to have been captured during a Crusade and having miraculous powers for the clan, and Rory Mor's drinking horn which holds the equivalent of two bottles of wine and which the bold Rory could sink in one go. Like the castle, they built them well in those days!

Those of Clan Donald returning to their roots will find a welcome in Armadale, on the Sleat peninsula in the south-west of Skye. At the award-winning 'Headship of the Gael' exhibition and Clan Donald Museum, is told the story of 1,300 years of the clan's history, particularly when the Gaelic nation flourished under Donald leadership. Carved in stone is the legend: 'Nih-eibhneas gan Chlainn Domhnaill . . . It is no joy without Clan Donald . . .' As at Dunvegan, there are walks to enjoy, restaurants for a relaxing meal and, most of all, a chance to understand the history of the island and its people.

Perhaps the most famous visitor to Skye was Charles Edward Louis Philip Casimir Stuart, Bonnie Prince Charlie. The story of why he was in many places in Scotland and the isles is well known, but the logistics of his crossing to Skye are these. In June 1746, fleeing from Government forces on South Uist and with a £30,000 price tag on his head, his supporters found refuge in the ruined castle on that island in Loch Boisdale. A plan was hatched to remove him to Skye, where he might be safer. Flora Macdonald was 24, well educated and had mixed with Edinburgh society. She sympathised with the Prince and his cause and was persuaded to take part in a devious plan. Her stepfather would pretend to be worried about her safety and send her to Skye with two retainers, a manservant, Neil McEachain, a Gaelic-speaker, and a maidservant, Betty Burke. This would be the Prince in disguise. Flora asked Charles to dress himself and he stripped off his own clothes – not his breeches, though – and dressed in a calico gown, a light-coloured, quilted petticoat and a mantle of dull camlet made after the Irish fashion. He kept adjusting his head-dress, cursing it lengthily, and wanted to carry a pistol under his petticoat. Flora suggested that it might give him away if searched, to which the Prince replied that if he was properly searched, it would not be the pistol that gave him away. They waited for a dark night, hugged the shore to North Uist and set off for Skye from Loch Maddy. Around midnight the sea roughened, which only raised the Prince's spirits and he began to sing. At dawn it was misty and they rowed into Loch Snizort where, after some argument, the Prince spent a night at the home of Lady Margaret MacDonald's factor, on the road to Portree. So he, like many before and since, had come over the sea. But early next morning, for me, it was out to sea.

At half past four, I staggered to the pier in Portree to meet Donald Gillies, skipper of the *Loch Innes*. He was going a-prawning and if I wanted to see how it was done, an early start was necessary. Up the east side of Trotternish, Raasay to starboard, past Prince Charlie's cave, Holm Island and the steps at the foot of the Storr Lochs Hydro-Electricity Power Station. The trawl was to be out for three hours, so it was a case of a cup of tea and a long wait. Early morning is a good time for the commercial boats, the first two or three hours of light often being fruitful. Donald was after prawns, but other species were picked up *en passant* and I was looking forward to seeing what these waters might produce. I'd taken a rod aboard, as Donald had promised an hour or two, after the work was done.

As the net came to the surface, there was not a bad catch. Prawns were graded into large and medium, with the small ones tailed into a third basket. There was a variety of flatties, plus cod, monkfish and a few small haddock. With the wind freshening and a fair swell, it was hard work to keep your balance as the *Loch Innes* wallowed in the waves. As the catch was cleaned, Donald headed for a mark to give the rods a bit of sport. The rocky coastline provides ample opportunity for the inshore angler but much of Skye's sea angling potential is unexploited, there being few boats concentrating on rod fishing. Pollack and coalfish are there and it is said that the whiting and haddock are coming back. Now, that would be lovely, wouldn't it? Haddock again. But we were catching some decent fish, good pollack and those lovely cod, iodiney-red from the kelp.

We moved in below the famous cliff-face known as Kilt Rock, where vertical columns of dolerite (a coarse-grained basalt) give the rock a pleated look. It was now fairly breezy and I had to use a loop of twine from under the chin and over the top to keep the bunnet from disappearing across the Sound of Raasay towards the Island of Rona – old friends must be looked after. The water from the Mealt Falls close by was being blown spectacularly all over the place by the strong wind and, as I suffer from vertigo, I was much happier on a pitching boat looking up than I would have been looking over the edge at the viewpoint, built out over the cliff. The water for the Falls comes from Loch Mealt, just over the Portree to Staffin road. An interesting wee loch this, reckoned to be unique in Europe in having no trout, only sticklebacks and char. The char were introduced as a source of food by monks who had a tiny monastery on the lochshore, but no one is quite sure where the sticklebacks came from. The char will sometimes come to a fly, usually something bright, silvery or gold, and are very pretty, green-bodied with yellowish dappling and white piping on the edges of the lower fins. We

The Falls of Lealt

The Diatomite mines think we are dashed smart these days, but the monks were at the fish-farming all those years ago – one cast of a net in the loch and the monks could gorge themselves on one of Nature's finest foods.

Not far from Mealt is Lealt, complete with falls and gorge. The Lealt River comes off Hartaval and Creag a' Lain and, as a fairly innocuous burn, under the road. It has then made its impression on the land, gouging the gorge and forming the falls. The way we got to the falls was breathtaking, in more ways than one – the view on the way down and the climb on the way back. As you take the path down, you look out over Rona towards Applecross and the mouth of Loch Torridon, almost to the spot where we caught those thornback rays, near Red Point. A quick descent takes you to the mouth of the Lealt and various buildings, a bothy, a netting station and remains of a diatomite processing plant. I looked up 'diatomite' in the dictionary: 'diatomaceous earth or kieselguhr, a powdery silicious deposit of diatom frustules'. I see.

Rounding the breast of the hill, you look back into the gorge and suddenly the falls are revealed. Someone described them to me as 'an awful black hole – you don't want to go there', but I thought it was really

162

beautiful as I walked up the short remnant of the river to the rim of the outflow with Neil Cameron, secretary of the Skye Angling Association. The water comes straight down about 60 feet into a large pool, sheer rock on three sides. Now, the river is short, and it is unlikely it can support many parr, yet salmon and sea trout are caught in the pool, most fresh-run and many sea-liced, the heaviest salmon caught being around 18 pounds. I wonder if these fish are using the pool as a stopping-off point, a familiarisation point on the way to – where? That said, some super fish come out of this watery hollow and Neil and I saw fish showing in lies on either edge of the apron of water below the falls.

You can sit happily on a ledge of rock and, with care, cast into the boil under the falls. I had started with a fly rod and worm, but couldn't get the bait into that meaty spot of white water, so changed to the spinner. Certainly better coverage, but no reaction from the fish. Neil had five minutes and, of course, did get a reaction – a double reaction, in fact. Interest from a fish and jealousy from me! A decent knock at the worm eventually produced a finnock; a herling, a whitling – whatever the name, it is a wee sea trout. We popped it back into the pool and fished on.

Neil felt our chances would have been better with more water. The pool fishes best when uncomfortable, a good spate tumbling over the edge of the fall being whipped by the vagaries of the wind into a froth that drenches the angler on the rock. But no such luck. Skye was dry, so no salmon. I was disappointed, but a trifle relieved. I would have felt really guilty watching Neil humph a big salmon all the way back to the top of the gorge. We might not have seen eye-to-eye as to why I'd come over the sea to Skye.

Chapter 17

FIFE AND KINROSS

Mary, Meadies and May

The secretary of a Scottish angling club is complaining about Loch Leven: 'The loch has been fishing poorly for a number of years, fish are small and the cost of a day's fishing is expensive. It does seem reasonable, though, to charge more for an evening session or when three anglers are in a boat.'

Does all this sound familiar? Well, that was actually back in 1934, when the cost of a boat was £1.75, the boat being £1 and the two boatmen, who had to row all day, getting the 75p between them.

The loch, with its beautiful silver-and-gold brown trout, has been the focal point of club angling in Scotland ever since 1880, when the first National Trout Fly Fishing Competition was held, making it the oldest in the world. Looking back over the years, it is interesting to see how catches fluctuated. In 1934, a poor season remember, the 62 national competitors landed 34 trout and the following year the same number of anglers had 687 – the two averages being about half a fish per rod one year and over 11 the next.

The history of the loch goes back to the end of the last Ice Age some 10,000 years ago. Retreating glaciers deposited sand and gravel in the area now bounded by the Forth and Tay estuaries and this low-lying ground filled with water to form a large shallow loch averaging three to four metres in depth, apart from several 'kettle holes' up to 25 metres, where huge remnant lumps of ice remained embedded in the loch floor.

The history of fishing goes back a long way, too. In 1314, King Robert I granted rights to the Abbot of Dunfermline to fish with 'one coble and two sets of nets', and by 1633 it was necessary to protect the stock from poachers, who were taking fish from the spawning streams. The proprietor even procured an Act of Parliament to that effect. Salmon and sea trout were running into the loch then, there was a market for the abundant eels, and char, perch and pike. All these fish, including the silvery brown trout, were netted for local consumption in the seventeenth and eighteenth centuries and further afield in the nineteenth, there being records of Loch Leven fish sold in Edinburgh and London.

In the early nineteenth century, the loch was larger and deeper than today. It was surrounded by marshes and a broader area that was susceptible to flooding in winter, a haven for waterfowl in huge variety. In 1830 a scheme was instituted to lower the loch by four to five feet, which involved cutting a channel from the loch to a point further downstream on the River Leven and installing sluices. This created new farmland and allowed better control of water levels to power various local mills. It was, however, less than successful. It took over two years to build; cost nine times the estimate; the extra farmland was not really required; weirs below the sluices put paid to the salmon and sea trout; and the eels, once supplying a quarter of the marketable fish (in the good years between 1865 and 1872, two and a half tons of eels a year went to market), couldn't make it through the pollution of the lower river; the char disappeared and the brown trout fishing diminished; the perch seemed to survive (a tasty meal for a trout, perch fry) and the pike were regularly netted, 2,000 pounds of them some years. So there was always a balance of fish in the loch until man, sadly, came along with his 'improvements'.

But in 1880 the anglers instituted their national rod fishing competition and since then the loch has always been an angling venue. It fished well until the Second World War, declined briefly, and then furnished a new generation with thrilling days until the 1960s and part of the 1970s. I had no quarrel with the loch in 1974, winning the National Championship! Since then, it has been in a period of flux, the water quality and trout feeding habits having been altered by the introduction of nutrients from farming, sewage and woollen-mill effluent. This culminated in the early 1990s in a dense algal bloom which made fishing almost

impossible and potentially dangerous. Schemes were introduced to remove the enriching nitrates and phosphates, and hopefully the loch will come back into condition. But in the dark days of the early 1990s, someone mentioned the unmentionable: should it be stocked with rainbow trout to give the anglers some sport until the brown trout fishing improved? Rainbows in Loch Leven? Anathema to some, a good idea to others.

Producer Ricky Walker with a beautiful Loch Leven trout

So, once again, I found myself at the end of a pipeline. It was mid-March 1993 and the first of the controversial rainbows were being put into the loch, along with the usual stocking of indigenous brown trout. Fed into a hopper beside the holding ponds, the fish slid down the pipe and tumbled into the water. The rainbows, hatched at the same time as the brown trout, were already substantially bigger as they swam off into the loch.

There was great interest as the season opened to see how the rainbow trout would adapt to the loch, but with such rich feeding there was little doubt they would thrive. I fished one evening in August with Willie Wilson, the fishery manager, and we soon had a chance to see for ourselves how well the fish had done. An acrobatic, aerobatic, beautifully conditioned rainbow came to the net. It weighed about a pound and a half, terrific growth in such a short time. We also had a natural Loch Leven brownie. The rainbows are good, but it has to be said that Mother Nature's naturally selected brown trout are unbeatable.

Of course, there are a number of other good fisheries in Fife and Kinross – Loch Fitty, for example. The season starts early, late February, and the weather can be nippy. I'm constantly amazed by the number of anglers willing to brave the elements at this time of year, but opening day is usually a sell-out well in advance. Summer evenings can be thrilling and frustrating, as fish rise to something you find impossible to imitate. All rainbows ain't easy, thankfully. Big fish come off Fitty each season and, with the splendid facilities at the loch, it has become an immensely popular fishery. Ballo Reservoir high in the Lomond Hills is another trout water that fishes well, as does Lindores near Newburgh and Cameron by St Andrews.

But the prize for invention surely goes to Lochore Meadows, 'The Meadies'. This country park near Lochgelly was created from a dark legacy of over 70 years of exploitation of coal. The pit bings, acres of slurry and waste and subsidence flooding have been imaginatively trans-formed into a facility for all the family. Lochore itself has three islands, Moss, Tod and Whaup, and is stocked with brown and rainbow trout. Boats are available for hire or you can bank fish and, a good move to encourage youngsters, bait fishing is allowed at certain times of the year. There is also a 'wheely boat', designed for wheelchair-users, and easy access round the loch for the disabled angler is another good feature. Parts of the loch are used for canoeing, sailing and windsurfing, there is a nature reserve, a self-guided nature trail and a stark reminder of the area's mining past is seen in the renovated winding-gear of the Mary Pit.

The Fife Ranger Service, based at the Park Centre, is there to help everyone to get the most from this excellent facility and I had an evening on the water with Chief Ranger Mark Wootton. He is a keen fisher and as part of his duties, well, he sometimes just has to try the fishing himself – a sort of Lone Ranger – but only to make sure the fish are of good quality, of course! There are some lovely drifts through the islands and a pleasant evening spent here is vindication of and a testament to the people whose vision created the park from that scar on the landscape, the legacy of Fife's industrial past.

But history and fishing go hand-in-hand in this part of Scotland. Dotted all along the East Neuk are picturesque fishing villages reflect-ing a strong sea-faring tradition. There is a special feel and look here:

whitewashed old houses with red pantiled roofs and crow-stepped gables. Others have styles imported from a long trading association with France, the Low Countries and Scandinavia, and many small harbours have fishing boats bobbing in the summer sun. Today, fewer boats operate commercially than in the past and many skippers find they can keep busy taking holidaymakers and anglers out for sightseeing and fishing trips.

On a day of bright sun, Jim Raeper eased the *Serenity* out of Anstruther Harbour, past the North Carr Lightship. It had been stationed near the dangerous North Carr rocks off Fife Ness until 1975 and is now in honourable retirement as a museum. It brought back memories of my Pirate Radio days with Radio Scotland ('242 metres on the Medium Wave'), aboard a similar craft, the *Comet*, anchored between the May Isle and the Bass Rock. Like the North Carr ship, we faced some heavy seas in the early months of 1966, but fortunately the 1993 sea was calm as we headed for a bit of ground not far offshore which rises from the sea-bed to form an underwater plateau. When running, the tide scours over it and it's an excellent place for cod. The fish were in co-operative mood and soon some plump, green-bodied cod were coming aboard.

Jim had asked us to keep a fish or two alive in a seawater-filled tub to restock the tanks in the Anstruther Fisheries Museum. This is housed in a group of buildings near the harbour and covers virtually every aspect of the fishing industry, both on and offshore – there being at least four jobs ashore to each man at sea and up to ten at the height of the herring season. There is an aquarium, where our cod were bound, and displays on the herring and the 'herrin' lassies' who followed the fishermen round the country, gutting, salting and barrelling the 'silver darlings'. Models of many traditional boats can be seen, like the Skaffie and the Fifie and the Zulu; whaling and commercial salmon fishing were important and are featured. A visit to the museum is a poignant reminder of the hardships people faced when making a living at sea.

As we brought our fish aboard, the birds wheeled round the boat and seemed to be calling for a share of the catch. There was a good variety of species, many of them from the nesting colonies on the Isle of May. I might have had a long connection with the Firth of Forth, but I had never visited this national nature reserve, so I was delighted when Jim suggested we take a look. The island is famous for its puffins and lighthouses, the first ever in Scotland being built here in 1636. As we approached the deceptive entrance to the tiny harbour, these comical birds were whirring and diving all over the place. Up the hill, over-looking the nesting sites on the precarious rocky ledges, we could see kit-tiwakes, fulmars, guillemots and razorbills in their hundreds. But no puffins. They were to be seen inland scurrying in and out of disused rabbit burrows, where they were feeding the chicks. After 30 to 40 days the parents desert the wee one, and about a week later it is forced to come out of the burrow through hunger. It then has to waddle down to the sea, usually at night to avoid hungry gulls, and create a life of its own. With their distinctive white face, red, blue and yellow bill and orange feet, they are unmistakable – and easy to see why puffins have also been called the 'sea parrot'.

Fife has so much to see and do that you'll be hard pushed to find enough time to enjoy a fraction of it. Back at Loch Leven, you can visit the castle where Mary, Queen of Scots, was imprisoned from June 1567 to May 1568. Here, she gave birth to still-born twins and abdicated the throne of Scotland in favour of her infant son, who became James VI and I. The details of her escape are well known: she was helped by Willie Douglas who, as he was serving at the table of her jailer, Sir William Douglas, dropped a napkin over the castle keys lying beside Sir William's plate. He then locked the castle and, as Mary was taken to shore, threw the keys into the water. I'll bet many an angler has wished he could hook that treasure while out fishing.

Try a visit to Falkland Palace, which dates back to 1539 and is another place connected with Mary, as she frequently hunted from there. The palace was visited by Charles I and Charles II, was occupied by Rob Roy after the Battle of Sheriffmuir and partly damaged by Cromwell's troops when they occupied the east wing. There are other historic houses – Kellie Castle, Hill of Tarvit and Earlshall Castle and Gardens to name a few giving an insight into Scotland's grand baronial past.

The Scottish Deer Centre near Cupar lets you get a close-up view of these fine Scottish animals and the St Andrews Sea Life Centre allows you to do the same with a wide variety of species of marine life.

St Andrews is, of course, a focus for the many thousands who visit Fife every year. Made a Royal Burgh in 1140, the town is imbued with history. The oldest university in Scotland was founded here in 1412, James V and Mary of Guise were married in the cathedral in 1559, and there are records of golf being played here as far back as 1547, though the Royal and Ancient Golf Club, the foremost in the world and the

ruling authority on the game, was not founded until 1754. John Knox preached here and Cardinal Beaton was murdered in the Castle in 1546. Though the town is steeped in things ancient, the modern visitor has every amenity: fine, well-appointed hotels and friendly guest-houses, a botanic garden, the Byre Theatre, some of the best weather in Britain (sunnier than Scarborough and drier than the Isle of Wight) and the world-famous golf courses.

Cleaning the bottom at Fitty

Just round the corner from St Andrews Bay's sandy beaches is the estuary of one of Fife's prettiest rivers, the Eden. Flowing through the Howe of Fife and Cupar to the sea at Guardbridge, this delightful water produces some big salmon every year, and, because it runs clear and in many places the banks are heavily tree-lined, it poses a few problems for the angler. Sandy MacIntosh fishes a particularly bonny part of the river near Springfield, on which he has done extensive work over a number of years, fashioning runs and pools from sluggish water and creating lies for fish.

As we walked the banks, he explained the fishing technique. It is a case of polaroids on, spot your fish but don't let them spot you. Once you have seen where the fish are lying, you can work out your tactics. The trees make it all but impossible to fly fish, so bait and spinning are the preferred methods. A small silver spoon cast upstream can work, as can the down-and-across approach. You tend to see the fish come for the lure and it is a real test of your fishing nerve not to pull the spinner away before it takes. It is even more exciting as you watch your couple of lob-worms wriggling in front of a salmon. Time and again it will let them sweep gently past its nose with complete disinterest. Sandy tells of fish that have picked up a bunch of worms lying in front of their noses and moved them to the side, as if telling them to get out of the way. Then suddenly, for no obvious reason on perhaps the twentieth cast, the fish will lunge forward and grab the worms. That's when the fun starts. The river is so narrow that the fish tend to shoot off fast and, with all the trees about, you sometimes have to get into the water to follow. Twenty-pounders have been caught from the Eden and my admiration goes out to any angler who can land a fish of that size from this water.

But we toiled in vain that day and it was on the way back down-stream that I met Iain Bayne, drummer with Runrig. Iain is a keen fisher *and* a Fifer and as I searched for excuses (too bright . . . not enough water . . . the usual pathetic cry of a fishless angler), Iain gave me hope. He suggested that Glasgow worms are not favoured by Fife fish on this water – local worms are better if you want to worm it. Of course! In a blinding flash it came to me. I did want to worm it, so I went to Wormit to get the worms to worm it. Seemed sensible, so that was how I came to be prowling with a torch in my hand on a dewy night, picking worms from the grass. It is a great way to get them, big glistening lobworms, a superb bait for salmon. They come to the surface on damp nights, but they are not daft. They keep their tails in the soil and are very sensitive to vibration and light. You have got to go carefully, not using the brightest part of the torch beam, and when you see a worm, you have to be pretty smart to grab it as near the ground as possible and pull gently. The tail will gradually come out and you pop it into a bait container lined with moss.

Well, I had been at it for just about 15 minutes when the police arrived. Someone from the local Neighbourhood Watch had reported that there was a suspicious man in their midst up to no good. Obviously *Hooked on Scotland* viewers, but the good men of the Fife Force realised it was a false alarm. In fact, they were quite fascinated by the whole process and even went so far as to give me a hand. Community policing at its best.

Back on the Eden, I was confident I was fishing the right bait – those Wormit worms, now under arrest in the bait bucket having been lifted by the police. Local Eden bailiff Ken Topping had seen fish, but the water was a bit clear. We tried here and there and I found it difficult not to spook the fish, although it was surprising how much they would put up with. Worms bouncing off their noses induced minor irritation and eventual resigned evacuation of the lie. But Ken had a spot in mind. Standing on the riverbank, there was a deep undercut below a couple of bushes which leant out into the river – an ideal spot for salmon to feel comfortable. Ken could see a fish in residence and, after a great deal of machination involving the rod point being poked through the bushes to get the right angle of dangle, he managed to get the bait to come into the lie every cast. The fish showed interest – a flashing turn telling Ken that it hadn't been spooked, rather the reverse. A few casts later it took and, after a spirited fight, I managed to net it for him. A late-season silvery fish, 6, maybe 7 pounds, it was just reward for the adaptability Ken had learned over the years he has fished the river. I defy those used to the wide open spaces of big rivers to imagine how difficult it is to fish a water like this. You have to be devilishly clever to tempt a salmon out of *this* garden of Eden.

Chapter 18

CAITHNESS

Watten, Wick and Wind

It is the fences that tell the story. No fine filigree of hedges here to separate the fields, but the solidity of slabs of Caithness flagstone set into the ground. Besides, natural hedges take a long time to grow in the northern winds and the stone gives better shelter to a new-born lamb and its mother on a windy spring day.

Like the lambs, we could have done with a few of those sheltering slabs out on Loch Watten, Iain Cormack and I. It was 3 May, a couple of days after the opening on the first, and the wind was brisk. 'Brisk', according to the dictionary means 'lively, full of life and spirit, invigorating'. Do not be misled. When applied to fishing conditions, especially in the north, it is an euphemism for 'a screaming wind from any direction, usually the wrong one for good fishing'. Watten is a loch with good feeding, about three miles long by half a mile wide, which opens later than many southern waters simply because it *is* exposed to those brisk Caithness winds, and over the years it has been found that fishing earlier is unproductive.

There are several other rich lochs on this plain of Caithness, including Heilan, Calder and Scarmclate. All have good fish in them and all can be difficult. But Watten we were fishing and as we started all was peace and light. The wind was fine as we laid onto a drift close along the

175

There are surprising places to visit in Caithness

south shore. A couple of natural rises gave us hope, but as another long cloud came over the sun, the wind changed and freshened and we found ourselves drifting out into the middle of the loch. As Watten is fairly shallow, and fish can be taken almost anywhere, this was no great problem, but it did make it difficult to plan our drifts. As a train to Wick rattled along the north shore, I rose a fish which put up a spirited fight. They are beautiful trout, Watten fish. Like Loch Levens, and some even say – sssh! – that Watten provided the first batch for the restocking of Loch Leven late last century. Be that as it may, in the net, I had to admire this trout. Golden-finned, spade-tailed and beautifully marked, it was about 10 ounces, just under the average weight.

The wind had now decided that it wanted to be even fresher and come from the south-east, so Iain, a regular and successful fisher here, suggested a drift near the Watten end, across the loch, past a point and round a small island. He knew what he was doing, too, as he took a similar fish to mine. We felt we had done well to catch anything with such a capricious wind and so early in the season, and as we thumped back over the rolling waves to the mooring, a fair amount of water came aboard.

Iain was soaked, but we bailed out the boat for the next anglers, relieved to be ashore again. I look forward to a perfect evening on Watten, high cloud, a set wind from the west and fish moving on the surface. A chance then, perhaps, to land one of the 3- and 4-pounders taken every year.

Caithness has over a hundred trout lochs, immensely varied in character. Out south-west, towards the Sutherland border and well into the flow country, are waters stuffed with wee (and not so wee) black (and not so black) brownies. Towards Forsinard, you'll find Skyline and Sletil, two excellent waters well known for quality fish, and many others have trout averaging three-quarters to a pound with the occasional bigger fish. And there are plenty where you can take a youngster or a non-angler and almost guarantee they will catch a fish. It won't be big, but if it is their first trout, it will be a milestone. And then there is Glutt, right in the middle of the moors. Many years ago, I fished this saucer of water with Mike Shepley. We had been told that there were good fish in this clear little loch and that evening was best. Mike was tackled up quicker than I, and, just as I was ready to start, he was into a fish. I netted it for him and went back to my preparations. Another shout, and I was netsman again. Three, I think he had before I managed a cast. These were big trout, too – pound and three-quarters to two and a bit – and in the gloaming, Mike put me to shame.

The most northerly lochs are those on the Dunnet promontory itself, the finest being Loch St John's. This is a well-looked-after water with high-quality trout. I've only fished here once, many years ago, and I can still see the only fish I caught that day coming to a dapping fly – a magnificently spotted trout of over a pound.

In nearby Dunnet, there is a little presbyterian church with a saddleback tower, possibly dating back to the fourteenth century. The minister here from 1601 to 1608 was Timothy Pont, one of Scotland's earliest cartographers. His surveys of Scotland were incorporated into Blaeu's famous Atlas of 1654, and are fascinating to look at nowadays. It always surprises me how accurate they are and it is interesting to see how place-names have changed over the years. For instance, if you go to the lighthouse at Dunnet Head, you are looking out over the Pentland Firth. Pont has it as 'Wenliknap Head' and the 'Pichtland Fyrth'.

Whatever the name, you are now at the most northerly point of the British mainland. At 346 feet above the sea and built in 1831, you feel the lighthouse must have seen it all. Days of idyllic calm, with barely a riffle to ruffle the surface of the sea, and days of nature in the raw. Strong tides – eight, nine, ten knots – being pushed by an opposing wind into mountains of water over the skerries. Even Timothy Pont noted 'contrarie tydes' off Stroma. Put simply, when the tide flows, the Atlantic funnels through the Firth into the North Sea, and on the ebb, the North Sea empties back into the Atlantic. This is genuinely one of the most dangerous stretches of water in the world, and we are not talking about a casual chat when the Merry Men o' Mey meet the Bores of Duncansby. Seen from John o' Groats, the Bores are created by a tide rip, with waves breaking over shallow water out to sea, and the Merry Men are a dramatic turbulence caused when the strong ebb tide rolls over the reef off St John's Point. The narrows between Stroma and the mainland, the Inner Sound, accelerate the water, and with a westerly wind fighting the tide, the Merry Men, dangerous dancing columns of water, can extend clear across the Firth to Tor Ness, on the south-western elbow of Hoy on Orkney.

> When the wild Men o' Mey in wind are at play,
> Let skipper and crew keep the boat well away,
> For each Merry Man is a most dangerous wave,
> And, caught in its thrall, no boat we can save.

An old verse on the Merry Men of Mey, which I have just made up, but nonetheless, these are highly dangerous waters for the mariner.

And potentially dangerous for the swimmer. It is doubtful if anyone would fancy a quick dip at the foot of Dunnet Head, too cold and too strong a tide, but if someone insisted, I think they might be dissuaded by telling them there are too many sharks. In the last few years, the waters below Dunnet and round by Briga Head have seen the capture of several memorable porbeagle sharks. The Caithness Sea Angling Club and the Big-Game Club of Scotland have successfully proved that big fish come close inshore at certain times of the year and can be taken on rod and line, with Dave Proudfoot of the Caithness Club landing a 350-pounder and Robert Richardson, a Big-Game member, boating a Scottish record 414-pounder.

By one of those little quirks of fate, Robert's fish was taken on 9 March 1992, and on 9 March 1993 Chris Bennet shattered that Scottish record, as well as the British, European and World records, with a fish of 507 pounds. Both these monsters were taken while fishing from the same boat, *Karen*, and that's why I was sitting chatting to Chris and skipper

Clair Calder about rubby-dubby. We were trying to catch a shark for the programme, but it was later in the year than they normally fished, and our chances were none too good. The theory is simple enough. You mash fish, fish heads, fish guts and fish oil in a drum until it is a pongy sludge, mix it with sand to take it down in the water, pile the whole lot into an onion bag and drop it slowly over the side (better still, get somebody else to do it!). The resultant fish-oil slick will work downtide and the fish should smell it and come to investigate. What it should find is a 3-pound coalfish bait attached to a long wire trace, all suspended from a balloon float. When Chris got the big one, the float only dipped briefly and he teased the bait back to the boat. The porbeagle turned and took it a few yards away, soaking those on deck with the power of its lunge at the bait. It was about half past five on a March evening. Chris had worked on shark boats off Cornwall and caught a fair number, so he knew he was up against a big one. It was a rough day and getting worse – darkness falling at six o'clock and the wind rising – as the fish headed north, in a six-knot tide, past Dunnet Head and out into the Firth. With Clair's skill at the wheel and Chris's determination – he firmly believes in letting the fish know who is the master – it was landed two hours and ten minutes later, almost six miles away, an amazing test of strength and ability. It took two hours to get back to Scrabster that evening, twice as long as normal, and, no fisherman's tale this time, they could not find scales big enough to weigh it on. The following day it weighed 507 pounds, but those who know reckoned it had lost between 5 and 10 per cent of its weight – 25 to 50 pounds.

Each year, a number of porbeagle sharks are taken here, but until more boats are willing to take anglers who are tackled correctly – mentally, physically and fishing-wise – we will not know just how many or few there are and when or why they come. Still, good for Chris and Clair – Scotland has one World Shark Record.

The fishing out from Scrabster is good; parties of anglers from all over Scotland and beyond come for a weekend or a week to try for the coalfish and pollack, the ling and the cod, and this was recognised when in August 1993, Caithness, through Thurso and Scrabster, hosted the European Sea Angling Championships. Over two hundred top anglers, from countries as diverse as Germany and Gibraltar, Switzerland, Sweden and, of course, Scotland, used all the guile and cunning at their disposal to try to win the coveted title of European Champions. Fishing was mostly pirking for cod and pollack and nobody does that better than the defending champions, Sweden. At the end of three hard days, they not only retained the title, but also had the individual winner in Jerry Svensson. I had been talking to him on the last day, once again aboard *Karen* and I was greatly fascinated by his style and attitude. Economical and confident, he *willed* the fish onto the hook. England were the runners-up and Scotland third. As well as the camaraderie of competition, it was a marvellous social event and many firm friendships were forged over a dram at night.

We could have done with a dram, too, one cool evening. I had joined Dave Proudfoot and several other members of the local sea angling association to try for a species that was previously uncommon in Scotland, the bass. This is a fish more usually associated with warmer southern waters, the Channel for instance, and no one I spoke to was sure why they are now found in these northern waters. Has the sea warmed by an odd degree or have the fish always been here? Have they had to move further afield to find food? Whatever the reason, they are caught from beaches all along the north coast and down to Helmsdale, just over the Sutherland border. We were on Sandside Bay, the white ball of Dounreay visible to the east. Fishing is best on an incoming evening tide with a good surf running. The fish come into the breaking waves and a tasty lugworm should do the trick. As the tide came in, we kept scrambling the gear further up the beach and one or two small flounders rattled the rod tops. Darkness fell and the lads lit the lamps. It was all very jolly, if cool, and that dram would have been welcome. So would a bass! Almost at packing-up time, I got a bite and landed probably the smallest bass ever caught in Britain. But it *was* a bass. Glinting silver in the lights, sharp-spined dorsal fin erect, it was a welcome sight. It may have been tiny, but it probably warmed me up more than any dram – though I had one anyway when we got back to Thurso. Just to make sure, you understand.

Some think Caithness austere, all open spaces and wind, but that is what I love about it. Acres of sky, ever changing with the wind, giving a wonderful variety of light, and like the lambs, you can always find a corner somewhere to shelter if you want. But if you are on the bank of the Thurso River in June when the salmon are running, the only shelter you'll want is the fishing hut for a quick bite of lunch.

This is the finest salmon river in Caithness, but not the only one. The Wick River has improved out of recognition in recent years due to the sterling work done by the local association, and permits are available.

The Forss, the Berriedale and the Dunbeath all have salmon and Loch Wester is one of the few Caithness waters with sea trout.

The Thurso is unusual in that it is controlled by one authority, Thurso Fisheries Ltd, and has been in the ownership of the Sinclair family for many generations. I chatted with the present Viscount Thurso, Robin Sinclair, beside the river at Halkirk and he spoke eloquently of what the river meant to him and what a large part it had played in his life and that of his family. He was wearing the kilt, too, bare-kneed – a brave move, as the midges were active. I was happier in the chestwaders – cowardly I know – but Lord Thurso took the wee devils in his stride.

The River Thurso has a mixture of water; fast streams, flowing pools and slow, deep stretches apparently without features, and all set in magnificent moorland. The river is divided into numbered beats, the anglers rotating daily downstream by two, fishing odd numbers one week and even the next. Stay for two consecutive weeks and you will fish the whole length of the river, roughly 25 miles, from Loch More to Thurso. Fishing starts early here, on 11 January, and springers, bright silver, glinting goldly in the peaty water, can be taken from opening day. But I was fishing in June and there were fresh fish in Loch Beg. This is not far below Loch More, which, until 1907, was where most of the Thurso salmon were caught. The then laird, Sir Tollemache Sinclair, decided to construct a dam at the loch to store water, and it was designed and built by P.D. Malloch of Perth, a famous figure in Scottish angling circles at the time. It was thought that releases of water in times of drought would encourage fish to run, but it has since been found that the water is best used to prolong a natural spate. Eddie McCarthie, the Thurso Estates manager, showed me how the sluices at the dam work, explained how judicious use of the sluice might gee-up fish in the top pools, wished me luck and left me to the tender mercies of Maurice Murray, good fun and fine ghillie.

Loch Beg has a run into it to die for. A gurgling stream, fishable with a short line from a wall of stones, spreads out into this mini-loch (*Beg* or *Beag* means 'small' in the Gaelic). But it holds fish. As the runs develop and more salmon reach the dam, those which can't get into Loch More (Gaelic for 'the Big Loch') drop back and this wee lochan is temporary home to good numbers of fish. I moved nothing at the neck, so Maurice suggested I wade the shore of Loch Beg, and with the floating line and a size 8 Black Shrimp, I was happy. If there was a fish to be taken,

Two Thurso salmon charmed out with the help of Maurice Murray

I was ready. Except I wasn't. As the river runs through the loch, there is a part where the fly works nicely, and as it comes out of that water, you have to hand-line. As you know, I don't know what to do when a fish takes a hand-lined fly. Stop? Keep drawing and pull the fly away from it? Panic, swear and drop the rod into the water?

But the Fates can be kind. With two cameras watching my every move, Ricky and Neville at the ready, Maurice at my side urging me on, a fish took. It did all the work and was on. A lively one, too, aiming for the Loch Beg reed-beds, boiling on the surface, shaking its head under the surface, it did all one would expect of a salmon. My heart was beating fast. This was what salmon fishing in Scotland was all about. The fish came close, Maurice slipped the net under a bright 9-pounder, and I could have kissed him. Have I got a thing about ghillies? Yes and no. The fish was fresh and silver and I was the only person in the world to have taken a fish at this time from this pool on this river on this day. At one point, the fish had jumped. In that thrilling mental still-frame were the mountains of Sutherland, visible across the rolling moorland of the flow country, the water droplets glinting in the Caithness light and the salmon

182

arching gracefully into the air. That moment is the essence of why I love the sport of fishing in this country, and it is why I am still, and will always be, hooked on Scotland.